Social Skills Training for Adolescents with General Moderate Learning Difficulties

Ursula Cornish and Fiona Ross

Jessica Kingsley Publishers
London and New York

First published in the United Kingdom in 2004
by Jessica Kingsley Publishers Ltd
116 Pentonville Road
London N1 9JB, England
and
29 West 35th Street, 10th fl.
New York, NY 10001-2299, USA
www.jkp.com

Copyright © Ursula Cornish and Fiona Ross 2004
Illustrations Copyright © Tiana Alexis 2004

Library of Congress Cataloging in Publication Data
A CIP catalog record for this book is available from the Library of Congress

British Library Cataloguing in Publication Data
A CIP catalogue record for this book is available from the British Library

ISBN 1 84310 179 3

Printed and Bound in Great Britain by
Athenaeum Press, Gateshead, Tyne and Wear

Contents

Preface

We have been working for several years with youngsters with general moderate learning difficulties. Difficulties in being included in mainstream schools in peer relations often isolated these youngsters from the rest of the group and acted as a barrier. We focused on developing various activities, together with the class teacher, to address the complex issues of relationships and their development.

Ursula worked with adolescents at a special school in London from 1986 onwards to explore ways of helping youngsters learn how to understand others, how to make friends and how to behave in a group of people in various settings.

Fiona, starting in 1995, continued running groups in the same school. The school requested these regular group sessions, and parents and students could see their benefit. Later Fiona worked with Dagmar Fabri, a clinical psychologist, adapting the group sessions to social skills training for young people with Asperger's Syndrome. At the end of the programme, some students were able to manage social situations better and were integrated into mainstream schools, while others felt more comfortable with their peers, and some dared to go shopping by themselves. All had fun and enjoyed coming to the group sessions.

The early work by Ursula was videoed and shared with the students as feedback and reinforcement. The sessions were based on a multi-sensory cognitive-behavioural approach that worked well in terms of improvement in students' behaviour in and out of class.

The success of these training programmes has been recognized by schools and participants but remains anecdotal. A more scientific evaluation of our work with students with general moderate learning difficulties is currently beyond the scope of our interventions.

The training described in this book is based on this success. It offers pre- and post- intervention evaluation schedules, interview and observation tools and specification of material such as tapes, in addition to ten detailed session plans that can be used and adapted by teachers to suit the special needs of their students.

The authors would like to thank the Marjory Kinnon School, London Borough of Hounslow, especially David Harris (the Headteacher), Terry Eccles and Lillian Smart (teachers in the project), and all the students who helped run the training and shape its format and content.

Note:

In most places in this book the pronoun 'he' is used to refer to a student and 'she' is used to refer to a teacher or Group Leader, for the sake of clarity. The information and exercises in the book remain equally applicable to and useful for children and adults of both genders.

Ursula Cornish
Senior Educational Psychologist
London Borough of Camden

Fiona Ross
Educational Psychologist
New York

Introduction

An important part of growing up is learning how to understand and behave with other people. This is necessary in order to be accepted and to cope in society. We have to learn conventions, how to greet others, what can be said, what should *not* be said, what is tactless and how best to interact with our fellow citizens. Part of growing up is acquiring conventions that help us to get on well with other people.

Behavioural problems in children are due by and large to some failure to learn to control their own behaviour and to comply with social norms. This is much harder for children with general moderate learning difficulties. This book provides a number of Social Skills Training (SST) sessions: aimed at 13–17-year-old students with moderate learning difficulties. The sessions have been shown to be useful.

An aspect of behaviour can be changed by the way we think about the behaviour and feelings associated with it. If we change the way we think about our behaviour, we can change the behaviour and act differently. This can happen through verbal mediation or through observation of other people's behaviour and learning from it. Behaviour is also influenced by its consequences, such as praise and reward or reprimand. The young child will learn to control temper tantrums and develop more socially acceptable strategies to achieve his or her aims. Most children who fail to control their temper and aggressive outbursts may be considered as showing maladapted responses to their frustrations, and these responses need to be corrected.

SST involves teaching new skills or correcting false patterns of behaviour and thinking. Inappropriate behaviour reflects an error or distortion in the thinking process of the child who exhibits the behaviour, so one has to teach the missing skills, such as problem-solving or self-instructional training or self-control. SST aims to teach individuals to be more precise and accurate in their information processing, and therefore includes cognitive restructuring. SST teaches the child to identify non-verbal and verbal social clues.

Psychological theory is based either on operant and classic conditioning paradigms or on an all-through cognitive mediation process, such as observational or vicarious learning. Much of a child's behaviour can also be under the control of internal speech or thoughts, as explored by Vygotsky (1962). Initially children's behaviour is controlled by external influences such as reward and punishment. As children grow older, they begin to use their own verbal instructions to guide their behaviour. Meichenbaum and Goodman (1971) developed techniques to teach children to gain greater control over their own behaviour by the use of self-talk.

SST can be used to improve problem-solving or help the individual to develop a better understanding of how to interpret other people's feelings and intentions and how to learn to discern the norms and conventions in a particular social situation. Milne and Spence (1987) outlined a programme to teach social perception skills, consisting of the following components:

1. Ability to analyze and recognize our feelings, identifying different feelings in situations that generate different emotions.

2. Sources of information that show how we feel (posture, facial expression, gesture and tone of voice).

3. Discussion and practice in decoding facial expressions, posture, gesture, tone of voice and social distance cues.

Methods include instructions and discussions, role-play, and pictures and audio-tapes. Children also need to learn about their own emotional states and recognize them in others.

Choice of Social Skills Training programmes

Literature describing recent research (Spence 1994; Spence and Donovan 1998) reveals that a wide range of SST programmes is now available for use in mainstream schools and with young adults. However, the choice available for young people with general moderate learning difficulties is slim. There are a number of difficulties in using currently available SST programmes with this particular group of children.

First, the literacy demands are often too high. A number of packages provide worksheets to be completed during the sessions or as follow-up homework. Both word-reading and comprehension skills need to be at a sufficiently high level for students to be able to complete these tasks. The required level is often beyond that attained by this group of students. Providing written responses can also be problematic for many of these students, and the effort to record answers can be demotivating. Furthermore, the focus of the task may be altered from that of learning a social skill to that of practising reading and spelling skills.

Second, students with significant learning difficulties invariably struggle with a high level of abstract conceptualization. Many of the concepts addressed in SST programmes are fundamentally abstract in nature, for example, recognition of feelings in the self and others, and understanding the relationship between feelings, events and interpersonal behaviour. However, in order to make such concepts meaningful to youngsters with learning difficulties, the method by which they are taught may need to be very different to that adopted for more able youngsters. Although the content needs to be similar, the process of learning must be adapted to their needs, making use of their more concrete thinking styles and drawing on their multiple intelligences (Gardner 1993). Examples of real life situations that form part of the youngster's daily experiences must be used wherever possible to illustrate the abstract concepts that define social skills.

Strategies for using Social Skills Training programmes

The aim of SST is to develop both the acquisition and the performance of social skills. For some youngsters, interfering behaviour 'gets in the way' of learning. Thus, teaching of new behaviour must be coupled with strategies to reduce unhelpful behaviour. Once new skills have been introduced, they need to be practised in 'real life' situations to ensure generalization. In short, training needs to equip students with the necessary discrete social skills and do so in a way that enables skills to be generalized and used effectively in social settings.

Many SST programmes incorporate both cognitive and behavioural problem-solving approaches. Cognitive approaches, such as problem-solving and decision-making, aim to ensure the appropriate performance of skills that form part of the student's repertoire, followed by generalization of these skills. In contrast, it can be argued that the behavioural approach is useful for teaching discrete aspects of social behaviour, such as making positive approaches to peers and giving and receiving compliments.

Behavioural approaches

Behavioural approaches use techniques such as modelling, rehearsal, feedback and reinforcement. Modelling can be live, or symbolic. Live modelling occurs when a student observes social behaviour in a naturalistic setting (e.g. a classroom) or in a clinical setting. Within school, a student's teacher is a crucial role model for social behaviour. The youngster observes the way in which the teacher greets students or the way in which he or she takes turns during a conversation. Although a teacher will model social behaviour unconsciously, she may wish to model at a conscious level behaviour that her students have difficulty with by drawing attention to the behaviour and the consequences.

A group of students, for example, has difficulty taking turns at a board game. The teacher joins in the game and models inappropriate behaviour, such as insisting on going first. She discusses the consequences with the students, who may respond by saying that it 'causes an argument with other players' or 'other players think she [the teacher] is unfriendly'. The teacher then models appropriate behaviour and again elicits the consequences from the students. If the teacher wishes to reinforce the appropriate behaviour further she may use symbolic modelling, where the child observes behaviour through a video or film format.

Rehearsal is another technique used in the behavioural approach. Rehearsal refers to practising a newly acquired behaviour in a structured situation such as role-playing, allowing feedback to be given. Target behaviour is positively reinforced through use of praise and rewards. Inappropriate behaviour may be reduced through skilful use of selective attention and negative reinforcement. Many children with significant learning difficulties can be taught discrete social skills (e.g. eye contact and smiling) through use of the above techniques.

Cognitive approaches

However, in order to apply these social skills successfully, deeper cognitive processing is required. Whilst at school a youngster encounters numerous social interactions each day. Interactions vary in their level of complexity, from a simple interaction such as a smile from the teacher, through to a complex interaction, such as joining in with an established playground game. In the latter situation the student has to decipher a number of 'social codes', such as whether or not to ask permission to join in and, if so, whom to ask. A behavioural approach relies on consistent stimuli in order to cue the appropriate behaviour. As social interactions are often complex and inconsistent, a person needs skills to make a 'best judgement' in order to navigate the social world successfully. An exhaustive behavioural programme would be needed to cover the full range of social dilemmas that a young person might encounter on a daily basis. A cognitive approach is arguably better suited to teaching skills such as judgement than a behavioural model. A number of respected social skills programmes indeed opt for a cognitive-behavioural approach. This aims to teach discrete skills and then ensure appropriate application of these skills in the real world by problem-solving, reading situations and reacting appropriately.

Cognitive strategies include coaching, self-control techniques and problem-solving. Problem-solving approaches promote skills such as identification of problems, goal setting, generating alternative solutions and considering possible consequences. In short, this type of training usually addresses:

- What is the problem?
- What can I do about it?
- Is it working?
- How did I do?

SST programmes for adolescents tend to assume that students have already developed an awareness of social norms, which can be used as a reference for identifying problem behaviour or situations. However, many youngsters with significant learning difficulties do not possess this frame of reference and thus struggle with the first step of a problem-solving approach – identification of the problem. As a result it is argued that, although cognitive-behavioural approaches should be incorporated into programmes for children with learning difficulties, a step prior to problem identification may need to be incorporated – that of developing a frame of reference for social norms.

Distinguishing between public and private

A sound frame of reference for what is 'public' and what constitutes 'private' is crucial for understanding the reasoning behind many of our social actions. Developing a concept of public versus private is often overlooked in programmes for adolescents as it is assumed that teenage students have already conceptualized both terms. However, students with general learning difficulties, who are functioning cognitively at a much earlier developmental stage, may not have made the basic distinction between the terms 'public' and 'private'. Thus, when returning to the problem-solving approach, a student who has not yet mastered the public/private distinction may fail to recognize that taking his socks off (a private act) in the supermarket (a public space) is inappropriate. He therefore struggles with the first part of the approach – identification of the problem situation.

Developing language skills

The language demands of cognitive techniques can be problematic for young people with learning difficulties. Cognitive strategies are fairly reliant on the use of verbal instruction to teach social skills and thus demand a certain level of cognitive and language development. Self-Instructional Training – a cognitive approach – clearly illustrates the need for adequately developed language skills in order for this technique to be effective. Self-Instructional Training teaches children to use self-control and problem-solving procedures to guide them through various cognitive steps. Usually an adult performs the task while talking out loud. The child is asked to perform the same task under the direction of the adult. The child then performs the task while instructing himself out loud. Next, the child is asked to whisper the instructions to himself while performing the task. Finally, the child performs the task whilst using silent, inner speech to guide his performance.

Coping with real life

With regard to the level of cognitive maturity of adolescents with general moderate learning difficulties, it is tempting to offer an SST programme designed for younger children, whose chronological age matches their level of cognitive maturity. However, a 15-year-old who is cognitively functioning at a 7-year level is likely to face many of the same social issues and dilemmas as his age-equivalent peers. Most adolescents with learning difficulties are not sheltered from issues such as attracting a girlfriend/boyfriend or from peer pressure to engage in forbidden activities such as smoking and drinking. If we aim to equip this group of young people to cope with 'real life' issues then these must form part of their training programme.

Need for practice

A further consideration to take into account is the pace of delivery of an SST programme. Although many programmes currently allow for repetition and overlearning of skills, this is often not to the extent that is required by students with learning difficulties. In order to ensure both mastery of a skill and generalization of its use across contexts, the student will require opportunities to practise that skill a number of times until it becomes part of his/her repertoire of social skills. To ensure generalization, there should be many opportunities for the student to practise the skill in at least the key settings in which it will most often be used. The student with learning difficulties is in particular need of a programme that allows for substantial overlearning and application in a range of settings.

Aims of the programme set out in this book

Devising social skills programmes for young people with significant learning difficulties thus provides an interesting and important challenge. The programme set out in this book is based on a cognitive-behavioural approach that has been carefully designed to teach relevant skills at a cognitively appropriate level. The programme teaches discrete skills through use of modelling, a high level of rehearsal, feedback and reinforcement. Problem-solving skills are taught in a highly structured manner and used to determine when and how to apply discrete skills. Social norms are explicitly taught, so that it is clear when a social situation needs 'problem-solving'.

In order to facilitate the transfer of learning outside the school environment, we have included homework sheets and a homework diary that can be collected in a homework folder and kept by the student. The homework diary is suggested for Sessions 6, 7 and 9. The idea is to reinforce the skill covered in the session and to apply it at home by documenting through drawings, writing (or, failing that, talking into a tape-recorder) with an adult about personal and interpersonal experiences. The recording of private and public thoughts will help consolidate a greater understanding about the appropriateness of particular behaviour in various contexts. Similarly, in Session 9, the diary can be used to record ways of recognizing and resolving conflict.

A further strong element in each session consists of parental/carer involvement. This helps the development of social compliance in students with general moderate learning difficulties by encouraging the family to become part of the programme.

National Curriculum Link

The programme outlined in this book is linked to the National Curriculum. The Personal, Social and Health Education (PSHE) and Citizenship Curriculum identifies four main strands for development:

- Self-Esteem

- Citizenship

- Healthy and Safe Lifestyle

- Relationships and Respect.

A number of the skills identified under each of these strands, at Key Stages 3 and 4, fit neatly into the current social skills programme. The main aims and skills that are addressed by the programme outlined in this book are summarized below.

Aims of this SST programme	Skills addressed in this SST programme
Increase self-awareness	Can recognize and name feelings. Is able to express positive things about self and others. Recognizes feelings in different situations. Manages emotions (anger, jealousy, excitement). Expresses feelings and recognizes impact on others.
Develop independence and responsibility	Completes simple tasks independently. Recognizes how behaviour affects others. Asks for permission. Is confident with new people and situations. Shows care for others and self. Is able to ask questions and to talk with adults about their thoughts and feelings. Can respond assertively to teasing and bullying.
Make the most of abilities	Recognizes what he/she is good at. Sets simple targets for him/herself.
Take active role in the community	Uses a range of approaches for decision-making. Resolves problems/conflicts democratically.
Maintain effective relationships	Can put self in others' shoes. Recognizes own and others' feelings, initiates friendships, is able to listen, support and to show care. Realizes that actions have consequences for self and others. Is honest. Voices differences of opinion sensitively. Says sorry and thank you and uses appropriately.
Respect differences	Recognizes worth in others. Makes positive statements about others. Shows respect by listening.

References

Gardner, H. (1993) *Multiple Intelligences: The Theory in Practice.* New York: Basic Books.

Meichenbaum, D. and Goodman, J. (1971) 'Training impulsive children to talk to themselves: a means of developing self control.' *Journal of Abnormal Psychology 77*, 115–126.

Milne, J. and Spence, S.H. (1987) 'Training social perception skills with primary school children: a cautionary note.' *Behavioural Psychotherapy 15*, 144–157.

Spence, S.H. (1994) 'Practitioner review: cognitive therapy with children and adolescents: from theory to practice.' *Journal of Child Psychology and Psychiatry 35*, 7, 1191–1228.

Spence, S.H. and Donovan, C. (1998) 'Interpersonal Problems.' In P. Graham (ed) *Cognitive-Behaviour Therapy for Children and Families.* Cambridge: Cambridge University Press.

Vygotsky, L. (1962) *Thought and Language.* New York: Wiley.

PART I

HOW TO START

Needs analysis

Setting up a Social Skills Training (SST) group for children with particular social skills difficulties requires careful planning. A useful way to start is by carrying out a needs analysis. This means gathering a picture of the skill set of each participant with regard to social skills development and defining areas of relative strength or difficulty. A person who is familiar with the participants in various contexts (such as a teacher, a parent or a peer) is in the best position to carry out a needs analysis. The aim is to define the areas of social and interpersonal skills that are not yet fully developed. These will help determine the direction that the programme should take. The following tools may be used to provide a clear picture of skills that need to be taught:

1. Social Skills Checklist

2. Interviews

3. Observations

4. Sociograms

Each is now described.

Social Skills Checklist

The Social Skills Checklist that we developed is closely matched with the requirements of the Curriculum for Personal, Social and Health Education and the Promotion of Good Citizenship for 12- to 14-year-olds (Key Stage 3). This stage of the Curriculum covers a range of skills that are important for coping socially in the wider environment, beyond the protection of a structured school setting. Thus Key Stage 3 was felt to be in line with the core aim of the current programme, namely to prepare students to be as functionally independent in society as possible.

The Social Skills Checklist probes different areas of social competence:

1. Attention (ability to focus and attend to others).

2. Reading social cues (ability to gain meaning from another person's social cues).

3.   Acting (ability to apply skills).

4.   Interacting (ability to read cues from others whilst monitoring own social behaviour).

To a large extent, the ability to focus and attend is crucial for appropriate development of the other skill areas. Attention skills (such as listening and eye contact) form the basis of more complex interactions, such as accurate reading of another person's social cues. Since a reasonable ability to attend is necessary for new skills to be learnt, attention is a core component of the current programme.

Clearly there is a high level of interdependence between the four areas of social competence defined in the Social Skills Checklist. Interacting, for example, demands both successful reading of social cues and an ability to apply skills. A basic interaction, such as a simple greeting, clearly illustrates use of these skill areas. A teacher enters the classroom, smiles and says, 'Good morning'. The student has to read the social cue as a friendly greeting and at the same time act upon it, giving a suitable response. An ability to attend is, of course, also necessary to ensure correct reading of social cues.

Why define categories of social competence if there is clearly such a high level of interdependence between discrete areas? By teasing out categories, a theme may emerge when assessing the social competencies of a young person. This will clearly help with structuring of the programme. A teacher is concerned about a student because of his/her difficulties with resolving disputes. At which point is the social communication breaking down for this student? By analyzing the student's ability to attend, read cues, act and interact, any specific areas of weakness in his/her skills repertoire may be teased out.

Underdevelopment or incorrect development of a skill can be considered both as a 'weakness' and as an area in need of support. Once areas of weakness have been identified, the impact that these areas have on the student's ability to resolve disputes can be analyzed. The Checklist may alternatively reveal that the skills needed for the student to deal with disputes appear to be well developed. The teacher should then look at external factors that may be hindering the student's success. Inappropriate responses from his/her peers or inconsistent implementation of behaviour guidelines in school could be external factors that are preventing him/her from resolving disagreements.

Ideally a member of staff who will subsequently be involved in the planning and running of the training (often the class teacher or form tutor) should administer the Checklist. This individual – or information-gatherer – should observe each child during a co-operative learning activity, to help inform his or her responses. Where possible the information-gatherer should observe each child in settings that involve co-operation with adults and peers, such as paired work in class or a group game. Opportunities to discuss each child's social skills profile with other significant adults (e.g. subject teachers, learning support staff and parents/carers) enable information to be gathered from a range of contexts. This shows whether an area of difficulty is specific to particular settings or is apparent across settings and helps inform choice of training sessions.

Administering the Social Skills Checklist

The Checklist is worked through before the SST programme commences in order to establish the pupil's needs. It provides a starting point for the ten sessions. It consists of 44 items that correspond to the levels of the PSHE Curriculum. As the Checklist progresses so does the increase in skill demanded as items move from Key Stage 2 to Key Stage 3 of the National Curriculum. Each item can be rated as 1 for 'always', 2 for 'sometimes' or 3 for 'hardly ever'. All items are closely related to the National Curriculum non-statutory framework for PSHE and Citizenship.

After adding up the total score, check whether the total is above 75. If so, it provides evidence that the person is lacking significantly in understanding other people or is inept in relating to them in an age-appropriate manner. The SST course would therefore probably be appropriate. Obviously this would need to be matched by observational data and parent/carer information as well as the youngster's view. It is important for the young person to want to take part in the course. Answers to individual questions in the Social Skills Checklist also help to point out specific strengths and weaknesses for that individual, and these should be noted.

Interviews

Interviews are an excellent means of gathering detailed information about a student's social skills and of clarifying any inconsistencies that have arisen in the Social Skills Checklist. Ideally time should be set aside to interview significant adults about each student due to start the SST programme. Significant adults may include parents, carers and teachers, particularly those who know the students well and have a good knowledge of their social behaviour. Where appropriate, peers may also be considered as they have a unique perspective on the social interactive behaviours of the student. However, the questions asked must be thought through with great care so that peers feel comfortable giving such information. In all interview situations it is crucial to have regard for privacy and to guarantee confidentiality. If the interviewee is unwilling to answer a question, their view should be fully respected.

Interviews can be unstructured or structured. An unstructured interview allows a particular area of concern to be discussed in depth. However, this may be at the expense of locating detailed information about other aspects of social functioning. A semistructured interview is a good compromise. It helps ensure that key areas are covered but also gives the interviewee relative freedom in the way in which they choose to respond to a question. The structure should enable the interviewer to gather a picture of the pupil's social competence, communication skills and empathy. An outline of a semistructured interview with parents and carers is given at the end of the Interviews section on page 26.

Social Skills Checklist

Checklist completed by:	Today's date:

Name of student:	Age of student:

The pupil shows skills in the following areas:

Specific skill area	Always	Sometimes	Hardly ever
1. Can describe his/her own feelings	1	2	3
2. Can demonstrate his/her own feelings	1	2	3
3. Is able to show what he/she is good at	1	2	3
4. Is able to say what he/she is good at	1	2	3
5. Says no to unreasonable demands	1	2	3
6. Understands that his/her behaviour has an effect on others (e.g. hurts others' feelings)	1	2	3
7. Knows what he/she can do well	1	2	3
8. Feels good about self	1	2	3
9. Is confident with new people	1	2	3
10. Able to share opinions	1	2	3
11. Knows right from wrong	1	2	3
12. Able to explain his/her views	1	2	3
13. Knows what is fair or unfair	1	2	3
14. Manages to control his/her feelings	1	2	3
15. Respects other people's feelings	1	2	3
16. Able to put himself/herself in someone else's shoes	1	2	3
17. Copes well with unforeseen change	1	2	3
18. Good listening skills	1	2	3

19. Pays attention to tone of voice	1	2	3
20. Pays attention to facial expression	1	2	3
21. Makes appropriate eye contact	1	2	3
22. Nods and smiles appropriately	1	2	3
23. Talks fluently using full sentences	1	2	3
24. Waits for his/her turn in conversations	1	2	3
25. Is popular in his/her class	1	2	3
26. Initiates contact with others easily	1	2	3
27. Able to 'read' situations	1	2	3
28. Helps others without being asked to do so	1	2	3
29. Works well with others	1	2	3
30. Takes initiative	1	2	3
31. Is a natural peace maker	1	2	3
32. Recognizes conflict	1	2	3
33. Able to resolve disputes	1	2	3
34. Knows actions have consequences	1	2	3
35. Knows how to deal with bullying	1	2	3
36. Knows how to cope with peer pressure	1	2	3
37. Able to resolve conflict through listening and accepting different view points	1	2	3
38. Knows how to help others	1	2	3
39. Shows care for others	1	2	3
40. Is confident with new situations	1	2	3
41. Knows what the appropriate behaviour is in different situations	1	2	3
42. Able to cope with fears and worries	1	2	3
43. Able to ask for support	1	2	3

Helpful tips for an interview with a parent (10–15 minutes)

- Create a relaxed atmosphere that allows parents/carers to share with you information about their child. Seating is important: a circular format is often less formidable than facing parents directly across a table.

- Try to keep the interviewers to a maximum of two so that parents do not feel overwhelmed or intimidated. As a general rule, just one course administrator should conduct the interview, unless there are concerns about safety issues.

- Tell parents the purpose of the interview prior to meeting them – i.e. it will serve as a way of finding out whether their child could benefit from participation in the SST programme. Give a broad outline of the programme, including the core aims and how it will be delivered, if this is known (e.g. ten small group sessions to be held at school during PSHE lessons). Ensure parents are aware that their child has been selected because he/she could benefit from increasing his/her independence skills and not because he/she is in some sort of trouble. Be positive about the child's social strengths and discuss how these might be developed further through access to the SST programme.

- Make sure parents know that you will treat all information about their child confidentially and that they do not have to answer a question if they feel uncomfortable with doing so.

- Ask open-ended questions to encourage the parent/carer to give full information and not the yes/no response given with closed questions, for example:

    'Does Billy have any friends at school?' (Closed question – lends itself to a yes/no response)

    'How do you think Billy is getting on with his classmates?' (Open-ended question – lends itself to a descriptive response)

  Examples of questions are given on pages 26 and 27.

- Ask parents to give concrete examples of any behavioural difficulties that they have noticed in their child. Try to determine whether this behaviour is problematic in all situations or is specific to particular settings, times of day, etc. Ask parents if they have any thoughts about what causes this behaviour. Do they have any ideas about how their child might be helped to overcome these difficulties?

- Encourage the parent/carer to use adjectives to describe the young person; it may be helpful to provide adjectives as a prompt. Check whether the youngster is described as outward going, boisterous, helpful, shy, 'lippy' with younger kids, scared of 'heavy-weights', etc.

- Ask in what ways parents/carers believe this youngster would benefit from taking part in learning about interpersonal relationships.

- Ask parents/carers if they think their child needs this social skills training and, if so, why.

Planning the interview

Prior to the interview, contact the parents/carers and explain the purpose of the meeting:

> 'The school is going to offer a Social Skills Training programme for a group of students. This aims to increase good social skills, helping students to cope successfully with daily social interactions. The programme builds on the many skills that the students already show. To find out whether your child would benefit from the programme, I need to understand more about his/her social behaviour at home. I would like to meet to talk further about his/her social skills.'

Conducting the interview

Start with a greeting and introduce yourself to the parents/carers. Ensure parents/carers are introduced to any other participants in the meeting (e.g. another colleague running the course). Welcome and thank parents/carers for taking time to meet you today.

Establish rapport by, for example, spending a few minutes talking about an area of mutual interest. Clarify the interview protocol by explaining that any information that parents/carers choose to offer will be treated confidentially and shared only with staff running the programme. Let parents/carers know that they do not have to answer a question if they feel uncomfortable in doing so. Re-check and confirm how much time you expect the meeting to take (in general the interview should not exceed one hour in length).

Gathering of information

Ask questions to gather a general picture of the youngster's social behaviour, interests and well-being. Begin with asking broader questions and gradually become more focused and specific. Prepare a few questions in advance.

Concluding the interview

Ask parents/carers if they have anything further to add about their child's social skills. Summarize the discussion to check your understanding of the main points. Let parents/carers know that you will contact them shortly, when it has been decided whether or not their child would benefit from the SST programme. Thank parents/carers for meeting you.

POSSIBLE QUESTIONS FOR PARENTS

Questions about social interaction

What does your child enjoy doing at home?

How does he/she get on with family members?

How does your child play with other children?

Can he/she share an activity?

Does your child make friends easily?

How does he/she behave when you have a visitor?

How does your child show that he/she is happy?

How does your child show feelings of anger/sadness/frustration?

Does he/she seek comfort/affection?

How does he/she respond to praise?

Does your child recognize feelings of sadness or frustration in others?

If so, how does he/she react?

Is he/she able to offer comfort/affection?

What happens when you tell your child that you are not happy with his/her behaviour?

Questions about social communication

Does your child respond when you call his/her name?

Can he/she follow single-step instructions?

What happens if you give multi-step instructions (carrying out two things at once: fetch a book from the shelf while you are getting my slippers from the bedroom)?

Does he/she initiate conversations?

Can he/she take turns in conversation?

How long can he/she maintain a conversation?

Does he/she show awareness of the listener and the situation, for example, by modifying his/her style or the topic of conversation or volume of voice?

Questions about self-esteem and confidence

Which adjectives do you think best describe how your child usually feels at home: happy, energetic, tired, irritable, sad, angry, excited, calm?

Can you think of any other adjectives that describe how your child often feels?

Does he/she talk to you about the things that he/she enjoys?

How does your child show that he/she is worried or upset?

Is your child proud of his/her achievements?

If so, how does he/she show this?

Does he/she like to try new things, e.g. visiting new places, or can this be worrying for him/her?

Is he/she willing to try something difficult?

How does your child view failures?

Can he/she view failures in a balanced and realistic way?

Does your child try to do any homework independently or does he/she usually ask for help?

Can he/she tolerate gentle teasing/joking?

How does your child respond to constructive criticism?

Does your child volunteer to help out at home?

How is your child with new people?

Is he/she outgoing or shy and reserved?

What does your child say about his/her future?

Questions about conflict resolution

Does your child often get into arguments?

If so, why do you think this is?

How is the argument usually resolved?

Does your child need help with resolving the argument?

What strategies does he/she have to help resolve an argument?

Can he/she calm himself/herself down after a dispute?

Observations

Direct observation offers a systematic method for gathering data about a student's behaviour in a particular environment. When planning an observation, first determine how it could help your assessment of the student. Did questions about the student's behaviour arise from a completed Checklist or from a parent/teacher Interview? Could an observation help answer these? The ways in which environmental factors impact on the student's social behaviour may be difficult to glean from a Checklist or Interview but may be made apparent through observation.

Two types of observation techniques are described here: running records and time interval sampling.

Running records

A running record is a description of events as they are taking place. Everything that is observed is included in the record, providing information that is helpful in analyzing the student's behaviour. Observations should be recorded as accurately and factually as possible, and the observer must be careful not to include her own judgements about what has happened. This method is especially useful if there are questions about how environmental factors impact on the student's social behaviour. By recording observations, the triggers or antecedents to a behaviour can be identified along with the consequences. An example of when and how to use a running record follows.

EXAMPLE OF RUNNING RECORD: SHAHIDA

Shahida is being considered for the SST programme as she has struggled to establish friendships in school. Ms Smith, her teacher, completed the Social Skills Checklist. Analysis of Ms Smith's responses indicated that Shahida rarely initiated contact with her peers. When interviewed about Shahida, Ms Smith commented: 'Shahida seems very shy and reserved. She doesn't much like group work and just sits quietly during a group activity. I'm concerned that she's vulnerable to peer pressure as she doesn't really stand up for herself.'

Shahida's parents, Mr and Mrs B, rated her quite differently on the Checklist. They described her as 'initiating contact with others easily' and as coping well with pressure from her siblings. In discussion they commented: 'Shahida loves having friends home from school. However, she can be quite bossy with them and likes to decide which game they'll play.' Mr and Mrs B were surprised that Shahida presented as shy and reserved at school. They did not perceive 'initiating contact with others' to be a difficulty for her and were thus unsure about the benefits of her attending the SST programme.

Phil, the programme administrator, decided that observation of Shahida in school would enable more detailed information to be gathered regarding her social interactions in the 'problem' setting. Phil chose the running record approach so that he could focus on the impact that environmental factors, such as seating and peer responses, might be having on her social interactions. His running record observation is given below.

PHIL'S RUNNING RECORD FOR SHAHIDA

Student: Shahida   **Setting: Classroom**

Date: 15 January   **Focus: Peer interactions**

10.20 Shahida comes back into class from PE with another girl, Rema. Their arms are linked. Shahida breaks away when she gets to her desk. Rema smiles and says, 'I've got chocolate milkshake for lunch.' Shahida smiles back then sits down at her desk. Rema walks away to her desk.

10.21 The teacher says, 'Please get out your project folders.' Shahida looks for hers in her desk. She gets out her pencil case instead and sorts this out. The teacher says, 'Shahida, please find your blue project folder.' Shahida follows the instruction, has another look in her desk and gets the folder out.

10.22 The teacher tells students to get into their project groups and to start making their maps. All students get up and move about the class. Shahida goes to her group table last. She doesn't have a seat but finds a spare one and moves it over to her group. She looks across to Rema who is at another table and smiles. Rema waves back.

10.23 Katy gets out the map for Shahida's group. She tells Tim to draw the roads and Shahida to colour the sea. Shahida goes back to her desk to get her colours.

10.24 Shahida stops at Rema's table on the way back to her desk. She whispers something to Rema. Then she asks Rema for a blue pencil. Rema gives Shahida all her colours.

10.25 Shahida goes back to her group. She starts colouring. Katy tells her to draw a boat. Shahida keeps colouring and doesn't answer Katy. Tim says, 'Yeah, a boat would be cool.' Shahida keeps looking at the map. She doesn't respond to Katy or Tim.

10.26 Katy asks Shahida if she likes to watch cartoons on TV. Tim says, 'I always watch them after school.' Katy says, 'My mum says I can only sometimes watch cartoons.' Shahida doesn't say anything.

10.27 Rema comes over to Shahida's table. She asks Shahida for a red colour. Shahida gives it to her and says, 'D'you like this map?' Rema says, 'Yes.'

Observer's comments

It seems that Shahida has developed a close friendship with Rema. She initiates little interaction with her other classmates, although she works co-operatively with them. This needs to be checked out with her teacher. Would SST be useful for expanding her friendship network?

Action following observation

Phil decides to check out his observations with Shahida's parents and teacher. He sets up a brief interview with all of them present. Phil feeds back his observations to both Shahida's parents and teacher and asks whether or not this behaviour seems typical of Shahida. Mr and Mrs B say that Shahida often talks about Rema and likes to ask her home to play. They commented that Shahida does not ask other friends from school back home. Ms Smith agreed that Shahida and Rema are especially close and that she did not realize how assertive Shahida could be with her friend. Despite this, all present at the meeting decided that the group would help Shahida expand her friendship network. She could learn to generalize her use of the interactive skills that she successfully employs with her siblings and with Rema.

ANALYZING RUNNING RECORDS

The SST staff may wish to carry out direct observation simply to gain a clearer picture of the students due to attend the SST programme. When analyzing the transcript they should look for evidence of social interactive behaviour, including the following:

- What is the quantity and quality of the student's verbal and non-verbal contact with his peers and his/her teacher?

- How does he/she react to requests, share material and share a joke?

- Is the student part of the group and does he/she seem to be liked by others?

- Is he/she withdrawn or assertive, demanding and/or attention-seeking?

- Does he/she make inappropriate comments or noises or laugh inappropriately?

- Is he/she relating to classmates or does he/she appear isolated?

By analyzing the transcript for social interactive behaviours, new and relevant information on the student's interactive skills can be gained.

Time Interval Sampling

Time Interval Sampling is an observation technique that involves recording specific behaviour over a set time period. It is especially effective for visible behaviour that occurs frequently. The idea is that the period of observation is divided into equal segments. Typically the observation will be 20 or 30 minutes long and will be divided into 20 or 30 one-minute segments. Each one-minute segment is divided into a 30-second observation period and a 30-second recording interval. The recording interval allows the observer to look away from the target student and make a note of his/her observation, i.e. whether or not the behaviour has occurred and if so how many times it has happened. The observer then goes back to the sequence of observing and recording until the observation period has finished. Time Interval Sampling also enables each student's behaviour to be compared with that of two or three other students who can be observed at the same time.

With regard to the current SST programme, this form of observation can be useful in a number of ways. First, a teacher may wish to find out more about a particular student's behaviour before recommending him/her for the programme. Pete, a Year 7 form tutor, has concerns about Dean's name-calling in class. However, he realizes that Dean has a loud voice and is unsure whether he actually name-calls significantly more often than his peers. Pete sets up a Time Interval Sampling observation to compare the frequency of Dean's name-calling with that of two randomly selected peers. Pete carries out his observation in the period during the day when Dean's name-calling seems most prolific.

Time Interval Sampling at one-minute intervals (30 seconds observation and 30 seconds recording)										
Behaviour observed: Name-calling Student: Dean										
	:00–:30	1:00–1:30	2:00–2:30	3:00–3:30	4:00–4:30	5:00–5:30	6:00–6:30	7:00–7:30	8:00–8:30	9:00–9:30
Dean	//	///	0	/	0	///	/	/	//	0
Grant	0	0	0	/	0	0	0	0	/	0
Rosy	0	//	0	0	/	0	0	0	0	0

From the observation it is clear that in this instance Dean name-calls significantly more frequently than a random sample of his peers.

Second, Time Interval Sampling can be useful for determining the success of an intervention. Let us suppose that a teacher wishes to implement the SST programme with three members of her class as she is concerned about these students' ability to listen to one another. In particular, she feels they find it hard to wait their turn to speak and frequently 'butt in' when someone else is speaking. She would like to gather a pre- and post-intervention measure of their behaviour with regard to the level of interruptions. Time Interval Sampling gives a concrete measure or score in which behaviour can be objectively compared before and after an intervention.

The Interview Sampling at one-minute intervals
(30 seconds observation and 30 seconds recording)

Behaviour a):	Abbreviation: ....
Behaviour b):	Abbreviation: ....

Student's first name	0:00–0:30	1:00–1:30	2:00–2:30	3:00–3:30	4:00–4:30	5:00–5:30	6:00–6:30	7:00–7:30	8:00–8:30	9:00–9:30	10:00–10:30	11:00–11:30	12:00–12:30	13:00–13:30	14:00–14:30

Sociograms

The decision to use an SST programme with a group of youngsters may be based on whether or not there is a need for friendship networks to be developed and expanded within a class. A particular need may be identified when a youngster or group of students in the class is isolated from the main body of their peers. On a day-by-day basis a teacher notices the general friendship patterns that exist between his/her students. A sociogram builds on these observations, providing the teacher with greater insight into pupils' perceptions of one another.

Questionnaire as basis for a sociogram

In the present context, a sociogram is the term used for a type of questionnaire (a Friendship Sheet) that asks students to identify others in their class or group with whom they like to associate. To elicit friendship patterns, questions such as, 'Whom do you like sitting next to in class?' and 'Whom do you like to be with?' are asked. If this form of questioning is cognitively too demanding for the target students, questions can be framed as simple statements, for example: 'I like to be with…' and 'I like to sit next to…'. Students are asked to complete the Friendship Sheet by themselves and to respond as honestly as possible. They are told that their responses will be treated confidentially and are asked not to share their answers with peers. See the end of the Sociogram section for an example, on page 36.

When the sociograms have been completed, the teacher can cross-reference each pupil's choice of partner for every question. This provides a detailed picture (a Friendship Network Grid) of the pattern of friendships that exist within the class or group. With such detailed information, it is possible to plan ahead with sessions in a way that promotes broader friendship networks. One of the key aims of the training is to help youngsters to be more inclusive of those who are 'socially isolated' within their class. Activities to support this are embedded in many areas of the programme. In particular, Session 10 directly addresses issues of friendship and inclusion. The sociogram can also be used to help measure the effectiveness of the training programme, in terms of expanding friendship networks. By administering it at the start and end of the programme, changes in friendship patterns can be detected. Is the child who was previously given no positive ratings from peers now given a few? Are there still some students who are not selected by any of their peers or is everyone chosen by someone?

Guidelines for use of the sociogram

Inform students that as part of the social skills project they are going to answer a few questions about whom they like to be with in school. It is important that they try to answer the questions by themselves and that they do not share their answers with another pupil. Let students know that their answers will be kept confidential and that only you (the teacher and whoever else is involved with the project) will find out what they have written. When students are ready and Friendship Sheets have been distributed, read out each question in turn, allowing enough time between questions for students to record their responses. Ensure that children with significant spelling or writing difficulties have an alternative recording method that still enables them to indicate their preferences. Collect the Friendship Sheets as soon as students have finished writing.

Script for administering the sociogram

Say: 'Today I am going to ask you some questions about your friendships at school. This will help me find out how our class can get along better.'

Say: 'Now I will give you each a Friendship Sheet.' (Hand out the sheets.)

Say: 'On this sheet there are sentences to finish about your friends. Choose students from this class for your answers. Write your answers in the spaces.'

Say: 'Don't show or tell anyone your answers. This is very important. I will collect your sheets at the end.'

Check that all students have understood the instructions so far.

Say: 'Now we can start. First write your name at the top of the page.'

Say: 'Read the instructions carefully.' (Read instructions out loud to students if necessary.)

Say: 'Go to number 1. This sentence says "I like to be with…" Now finish the sentence.' (If necessary, give an example such as 'I like to be with Milly' – choose a named member of the class.)

Say: 'Write your answer in the blank space.' (Check that students have finished writing before going on to the next question.)

Say: 'Go to number 2. This sentence says "In class I like to sit next to…" Now finish the sentence.'

Say: 'Go to number 3. This sentence says "I like to share my things with…" Now finish the sentence.'

Say: 'Well done. You have finished. I will collect your sheets. Remember to keep your answers to yourself.'

An example of a Friendship Sheet is now given and may be photocopied for class use.

Friends

My name is

This sheet is to help find out which classmates you like to spend time with. Think of all the people in your class. Now choose who you would like to do each of the activities below with. You can't choose someone from another class, but it is OK to pick someone from your class who is away from school today. You can choose boys or girls. Try to fill in every space. Please do not talk about your choices with your classmates.

(1) I like to be with

(2) I like to sit next to

(3) I like to share my things with

Usefulness of Friendship Network Grid

Use the Friendship Network Grid that follows to analyze pupil responses. A completed example is given, followed by a blank version that Leaders may photocopy for use in their own groups. Highlight any students in the group who have not been selected by any other. When the sociograms (Friendship Sheets) are administered again at the end of the programme it will be possible to compare numbers of children who have not been given a rating at the start and at the end of the programme. This will help determine the effectiveness of the programme as a means of expanding and developing friendship networks within this class or group. At the same time it will serve as a means of evaluating the programme by comparing pre- and post-training choices to the same set of questions.

Example of a Friendship Network Grid

Date of completed Network Grid: 12.11.2001

Student year group: 9 and 10

This worked example is based on Question 1 from a Friendship Sheet (I like to be with…)

Response to Question 1: x indicates choice made by each student

	Sean	Rim	Tom	Che	Sha	Pat	Jo	Ka
Sean			x					
Rim				x				
Tom								x
Che								x
Sha			x					
Pat		x						
Jo			x					
Ka					x			

From this grid we can see that Sean has indicated that he likes to be with Tom, Rim has indicated that she likes to be with Che and so on. Tom has been selected the most times as a person that others like to be with. Two students, Pat and Jo, have not been selected at all.

Friendship Network Grid

Date of completed Network Grid:

Student year group:

Question:

Name								

PART 2

THE TRAINING
PROGRAMME

Introduction: Planning the sessions

The training programme consists of ten sessions, each with a homework assignment to be completed the following week. The content of the ten sessions is a reflection of the core social skills covered in the PSHE Curriculum. These are broadly as follows:

1. Listening and paying attention

2. Monitoring spoken language – paying attention to tone of voice and to turn-taking

3. Monitoring body language in ourselves and reading body language in others

4. Recognizing own and others' strengths

5. Learning to say no to unreasonable demands and to cope with peer pressure

6. Recognizing and describing own and others' feelings

7. Learning to control own feelings

8. Being confident to explain own views and to ask for support when needed

9. Recognizing and learning to resolve conflict

10. Showing care and concern for others.

Each session has a primary focus on a particular skill, which is emphasized in the activities provided and the suggested role-play scenarios. It is not necessary to follow sessions in the order in which they are presented in this book, and it is anticipated that sessions will be selected according to need. Furthermore, the sessions provide a useful framework to which Administrators can add their own ideas and make alterations according to the needs of their group. Finally, there are opportunities to reinforce concepts by including the consolidation sessions in the programme. Consolidation sessions are repetitions of previously introduced skills in order to allow for overlearning.

Central themes underpin all the sessions and are viewed as fundamental to successful social integration. These themes have the implicit aim of helping students develop in the following areas: tolerance of other people; ability to identify and respect other people's feelings; awareness that our own actions have consequences; and confidence to ask for help when required.

Owing to the need for overlearning and repetition for students with moderate general learning difficulties, it is best to focus on developing a few skills that are relevant to the group as a whole rather than a wide range of skills. In this way key skills can be revisited on several occasions in different contexts, allowing for their generalization and consolidation. Use the information gathered on each student to draw out common themes or threads that present as areas of need for the group as a whole. These themes can then be matched with appropriate sessions from the book, e.g. if turn-taking is an area of difficulty for several students in the group, Session 2 could be considered.

Session format

To enable students to become familiar with the programme, sessions follow a similar format. This is as follows:

1. Welcome to group

2. Recap on previous sessions and on any homework set

3. Warm-up activity

4. Introduction to this week's topic and activity focusing on skills linked to topic

5. Role-play and discussion

6. Closing activity

7. Giving compliments

8. Setting homework

9. Ending session

The ideal group size is between six and ten students with two adults present (such as the class teacher and a learning support assistant). In this book the two adults are referred to as the Group Leaders, or Leaders, to help distinguish between students and teachers. However, in practice the Leaders should use their usual titles. Many of the activities are designed so that Leaders can participate alongside their students. Leaders can role-model activities in this way and keep up motivation and pace.

Physical organization

The room should be arranged so that participants are sitting in a circle at the start of each session. Have students seated on chairs rather than on the floor to ensure that they are comfortable. Activities during the middle part of a session will often require students to work in small groups, pairs or individually, so be prepared for desk and chair re-shuffling. Each session should end with students sitting back in a circle, enabling opportunities for discussion and for whole group closing activities.

Communication with parents, carers and teachers

To ensure that skills learnt in each session are practised in the 'real world', allowing for generalization, a brief letter to parents can be sent at the end of each session. A sample letter is provided at the end of each of the ten sessions in this book. This letter outlines the content of the session, the specific skills addressed and a task that can be carried out at home ('homework') to reinforce learning of the target skills. A space is provided at the end of each sample letter for parents to record their observations of how the child has managed the homework task(s) or applied the target skills in other contexts.

Timing of each session

Each session should last about 100 minutes. Within each session, there are frequent changes of activities, with most lasting about 10 minutes, except for the role-play section which is usually the longest at 25–30 minutes. The students normally keep up their concentration and can follow the whole session without a break. The teacher will have to decide how well the group can cope with the length of time, and may if necessary decide to build a 15-minute break into the session. The drawback of including a break is the loss of momentum and general focus of the whole session. The students may lose the thread. In general teenagers can cope well with the length of sessions, given that they include such diverse and interactive elements as observation, listening, talking, drawing and acting.

Session 1

Target area: Listening and paying attention (Skill Area 1)

Session aims and preparation

Key learning aims

Students: Develop a concept of good listening skills, understanding the difference between good and bad listening

Start to listen actively to other people, paying attention to what they are saying

Show good listening by providing relevant responses to questions or comments

General aims

Students: Begin to feel relaxed in the group setting

Learn the names of other participants, if there are unfamiliar pupils (e.g. from a different class) in the group

Have fun

Link area of PSHE and Citizenship Curriculum

Students build effective relationships by developing listening skills

Materials needed

Beanbag, tape recorder, sounds tape (any commercially available tape with sound effects will do), Pupil Compliments Sheets (ideally A2-sized pieces of white paper)

Suggested additional materials

Hats and scarves for role-play

Session plan

1. Welcome and introduction to the group (10–20 minutes)

Only include this part of the session if this is the first group meeting with the students. Part 1 may be used at the start of any other session in which the group is meeting for the first time.

Group organization: students and Group Leaders are seated on chairs arranged in a circle. Welcome and introduce the group as follows:

- Tell students that we are going to meet each week (or as arranged) as a group to practise our social skills.

- Find out what students understand by 'social skills'. Encourage them to think of the different things they learn at school – maths, reading, spelling, etc. Do they learn anything else? Help students also to think about school as a place where we learn to make friends, to work with other people and to share games. These things are all to do with social skills. Tell students that by joining in with the sessions they will practise getting even better at these things. Social skills are important for getting on in school and also for getting on with people outside of school.

- Tell students that this is a special group where people can try new things without feeling embarrassed, shy or silly. We can be helpful to each other by not laughing and teasing when someone tries something new. Sometimes a group member may want to share a special thought just with the group. We should not talk about this after the group has finished. The Leaders will only share private information outside the group if they are seriously worried that something a group member has said may be harmful to the youngster him/herself or others.

- Provide students with a broad structure for the sessions. Display a session plan clearly in the room so that all students can see it. This could be written on the board if students are able to read. If not, draw simple pictures or symbols to illustrate the different parts of each session. Run through the schedule. Point to the different activities as you say the following (or similar):

  'Each session starts with a welcome and a warm-up activity. Then we will look at any homework that you have done. Next we will talk about the skills to learn this session, play some games and do some acting or role-play to practise these skills. At the end of the session we will think about what other people in the group have done well (compliments) and find out about the new homework.'

Cross out each activity after it has been completed so that students keep track of what they have done and are aware of what to expect next.

Warm-up activity (10 minutes maximum)

ACTIVITY: BEANBAG GAME (GETTING TO KNOW EACH OTHER)

Materials: one colourful beanbag
Group organization: students and Group Leaders standing in a circle

Students and Group Leaders each take turns to say their name out loud. Then students and Leaders take turns at throwing the beanbag to one another, in a random order. As a person throws the beanbag, they say their own name out loud. Continue until all group members have had at least one or two goes at throwing and catching the beanbag.

2. Recap on the previous session and on any homework (10 minutes)

Skip this if this is the first session.

3. Introduction to this week's topic (10 minutes maximum)

Group organization: students and Group Leaders are seated on chairs arranged in a circle.

Explain to students that as we grow up we need to develop special skills and ways to help us get on well with our family, friends and all the other people we meet. These special skills include communication. Ask students what they understand by communication. Encourage and prompt responses such as: being able to listen, to understand, to explain things, to follow instructions and hear people's ideas. Tell students that today we will work on our 'listening' skills.

4. Topic-linked activities: listening games (20 minutes maximum)

Depending on time and need for reinforcement, select two, three or all four activities.

ACTIVITY A: WHAT'S THAT SOUND?

Materials: sounds tape – side 1
Group organization: circular seating

Ask students to listen very carefully to the different sounds on the tape. Explain that you will stop the tape after each sound and ask students to tell you what they have heard. Examples of sounds might be running water and a dog bark. At the end of the tape ask students what they needed to do to guess the right sound. Encourage responses such as 'sit still', 'listen', and 'not talk'.

ACTIVITY B: CHATTER BOX!

Materials: sounds tape – side 2
Group organization: circular seating

Can you listen and talk at the same time?

Tell students they are going to hear a tape. (Note: This tape is a suggested example. Teachers can adapt it depending on what sounds tape they have.) There will be people talking about their pets. When you first play the tape ask children, in pairs, to talk to each other. They can just say apples and oranges to each other if they want. At the end of the first dog description, ask children what they found out about the person's dog. How easy was it to listen? What made it hard for them to listen well? Encourage response: 'talking to someone made it hard'.

Now play the second animal description (cat). Ask children to walk around the room as you play it. What did they find out about the cat? Did they remember everything the owner said about her cat? What made it hard for them to listen well? Encourage response: 'walking or moving about / not sitting still made it harder to listen'.

Play the third animal description (rabbit). Ask students to sit still and to try to listen well. They must not talk to other people while the tape is playing. What did they find out about the rabbit?

Did they find out more about the pet when they were listening well?

ACTIVITY C: WHAT'S NEXT?

Materials: questions to read
Group organization: circular seating

Tell students you are going to say some sentences with the end missing. Their job is to listen carefully to each sentence, then make up a sensible ending for it. After each sentence ask for suggestions from students. At the end of the game ask students what they needed to do to make a good ending. Encourage responses such as: 'listen to what was being said'.

Questions to read:

- ° Jim went to the fruit shop and bought an apple, some pears and some...
- ° When Kim's at home she likes to read a book, watch television and...
- ° John's favourite colour is...
- ° Today Kit had a tasty lunch at school. She had...
- ° Jack did not have a good day yesterday. In the morning he fell off my bike and in the afternoon he...

ACTIVITY D: ODD ONE OUT

Materials: word list
Group organization: circular seating

Tell students that you are going to say the names of three things. They must listen carefully to what you say. Their job is to work out which word does not fit with the others. Here is an example. Say 'apples, pencils, oranges'. Ask, 'Which is the odd one out or doesn't fit?' (answer – pencils). When students are sure of the game, continue with the following word groups:

dog, sun, cat	**book, red, yellow**
boy, girl, monkey	**chair, banana, table**
cup, shoe, sock	**lemonade, water, box**
wheel, box, ball	**chocolate, cake, mud**
nice, pretty, monster	**run, jump, elephant**

At the end of the game ask students what skills they needed for this game. Encourage responses about good listening skills.

5. Role-play/drama (25–30 minutes)

- Tell students that we are going to do some drama. Explain to, or remind students that in drama we pretend to be different people and that sometimes we will pretend to be in a different place to the classroom.

- Ideally, if this is the first role-play for the group, the two Leaders can take on the roles of the two characters: Miss (or Mr) Miller, who is trying to tell a story (e.g. what happened when she or he lost a purse), and Miss (or Mr) Smith, who keeps interrupting (shouting out, waving hands, turning back on speaker, etc.). Tell students that we (the Leaders) are going to pretend to be Miss Miller and Miss Smith. Ask them to watch carefully to see what is wrong with Miss Smith's behaviour. Tell students that they must wait until the end of the drama before saying what they think is wrong. You may wish to emphasize to students to observe how well Miss Smith is listening. Miss Miller and Miss Smith wear hats/scarves to reinforce the idea of role-play/drama.

- If there is time, and if you feel students are confident enough to attempt role-play at this stage, encourage them to act out in pairs being Miss or Mr Miller and Miss or Mr Smith. Ask pupils who took on the role of Miss or Mr Miller how they felt. Did they like speaking to Miss/Mr Smith? If not, why not? Did they start to feel annoyed or cross when they were not being listened to?

6. Group discussion (10 minutes)

- At the end of the role-play, ask students about Miss Smith's behaviour. Encourage them to answer the following questions:

  'Was Miss Smith showing good or bad listening?'

  'What makes you think that?'

  'What happened when she interrupted Miss Miller?'

  Try to include the following points in the discussion: you don't hear the other person properly; you may miss an important message; you may be thought of as rude or not interested.

- Record answers on a board/flip chart so you can revisit the students' answers in future sessions.

7. Closing game (5–8 minutes)

ACTIVITY: CHINESE WHISPERS

Materials: none needed

Group organization: circular seating

Make sure all students are sitting in a circle. One of the Leaders starts off by whispering a message to the person on her right, such as, 'Fish fingers are my favourite food', and asks the person on her right to whisper the message to the next person along. When the message has travelled the circle, the last person to receive it (i.e. the person on the Leader's left) says out loud the message that he or she has heard. Was it the same as the Leader's message?

Quick discussion – ask: 'Did the message change along the way? If so why did it change?' Help students recognize that we need to listen very carefully to hear exactly what someone says.

8. Compliments (5 minutes)

Display a large A2-sized (or similar) sheet of white paper for each pupil around the group room. The pupil's name needs to be written at the top of their sheet. Find a way to pin up and take down the sheets of paper easily as they will be redisplayed around the group room each session. With students still sitting in a circle, ask each person to give a compliment about the student sitting on their left – something that person has done well in this session, or more generally in school. This might include, for example, 'giving good answers', 'joining in role-play', 'sitting still', 'sharing pencils in class'. While compliments are being given, record them on the sheet of the person being complimented. This provides a record of achievement (as seen by peers) and should go a long way to raising pupil self-esteem.

9. Homework (8 minutes)

Tell students that during the coming week we will practise good listening skills at school and at home. Give students a copy of the Good Listening Prompt Sheet (it may be useful to provide one for school and one for home). Tell students to put their Prompt Sheets in a place where they can easily see them (e.g. taped to desks or to the fridge at home). Ask them to look at their Prompt Sheet during the week to help remember the good listening skills learnt. Let students know we will talk about how they have managed 'good listening' in the second session.

10. End session

Thank and congratulate students for completing the session.

HOMEWORK SHEET 1.1: GOOD LISTENING PROMPT SHEET

Sometimes we listen when people talk to us, and at other times we don't listen. Look at the way the people are sitting or standing in these pictures. Are they facing each other? Look at what they are doing with their hands. Can you tell which of these people are listening well? Mark with a tick each person who is listening well.

Model letter to parents/carers at the end of Session 1: Listening and paying attention

Date:

Dear Parents/Carers,

The social skills group has just been learning about listening and paying attention. In this session we discovered the difference between good and bad listening and practised active listening. Students played games where they were asked to chat to each other or walk about the room whilst being played a tape of a person speaking. They found out how much easier it is to hear and remember what someone says if you sit still and actively listen to them. Our role-play followed this theme and illustrated how 'bad listening' affects both the speaker and the listener. The speaker may feel annoyed, unhappy or cross that he or she is not being listened to. The listener is likely to miss out on important information.

For homework this week, students have been asked to practise their good listening skills. Your child will bring home a 'Good Listening Prompt Sheet'. This has several illustrations outlining the do's and don'ts of good listening. Please share this sheet with your child and ask him or her to tell you about the different illustrations. Then display the sheet in a place where it can be easily seen, such as on the fridge door. Over the week, take care to point out any examples of good listening that your child shows. Praise your child for his or her efforts and try to model good listening in return.

Thanks for your help with the programme. You are a very important part of it, and your support will make a difference.

Best wishes,

Names of Course Leaders

- - - - - - - - - - - - ✂ -

Dear Parents/Carers, please complete this section and return it with your child when he/she attends the next session.
How did your child manage the homework?

How would you now rate his/her listening and turn-taking skills at home?

☐ Has a lot of difficulty   ☐ Has some difficulty   ☐ Has a little difficulty   ☐ No difficulty

Session 2

Target area: Listening and turn-taking (Skill Areas 1 and 2)

Session aims and preparation

Key learning aims

Students: Demonstrate active listening skills by giving relevant responses to questions and comments

Develop further reciprocity of conversation (turn-taking skills)

General aims

Students: Feel relaxed in the group setting

Learn the names of other participants, if there are unfamiliar pupils (e.g. from a different class) in the group

Have fun in the group

Link area of PSHE and Citizenship Curriculum

Students build effective relationships through being able to listen to others and to recognize feelings in others. Students develop independence and responsibility by recognizing how their own behaviour affects others.

Materials needed

Beanbag, colouring sheets for each pupil and model coloured sheets prepared by teacher, colouring pencils, Pupil Compliments Sheets

Suggested additional materials

Hats and scarves for role-play

Session plan

1. Welcome to the group and warm-up activity (5–8 minutes)

Group organization: students and Group Leaders are seated on chairs arranged in a circle. Tables are to be arranged outside the circle to be available for the turn-taking game.

Start this session with a round of the beanbag game (see warm-up activity in Session 1), providing a fun and familiar warm-up activity.

2. Recap on the previous session and on any homework set (8–10 minutes)

If the previous session was Session 1, use the following questions for discussion:

- What did we learn last session?
- Did you use your prompt sheet and where did you put it?
- Which skills on the sheet did you do better at?
- What happened when you listened better?
- Did anyone notice your good listening, such as a parent, friend or teacher?

If the previous was a session other than Session 1, use questions from that session to guide a group discussion.

3. Introduction to this week's topic (8–10 minutes)

Remind students that as we grow up we need to develop special skills to help us get on well with our family, friends and all the other people we meet. These special skills include communication. Ask students what they remember about communication. Encourage and prompt responses such as good listening, talking and looking. Tell students that today we will work on our 'listening' skills, just as we did in the last session. As well as practising good listening we will also find out about turn-taking. Remind students about issues of confidentiality, i.e. keeping information that students share within the class.

4. Topic-linked activity: turn-taking game (10 minutes)

ACTIVITY: COLOUR CHALLENGE!

Materials: coloured version of picture (two, i.e. one per table), photocopied and uncoloured version of picture (one per student), two pots of coloured pencils (each pot must contain just one of every colour needed to complete the picture).

Group organization: students should be organized into two, preferably even-sized, groups for this activity and to be seated around two tables.

Hand each student a photocopy of the drawing that has not been coloured in. Then show the two groups the coloured version of the drawing and place a copy of it in the centre of each of the two tables. Place on both tables a pot of pencils. Each pot must contain one of every colour that is shown in the drawing. Say to students: 'Your job is to colour your picture just like the one in the middle of the table. You can use the pencils in the pot but cannot use any others. That means you have to share the pencils with the other students on your table. There is a tricky challenge! You are *not allowed to speak during this activity.* So you must share the pencils without talking. The aim is for everyone in your group to have their picture coloured in under five minutes. So remember to work as a team and to look out for each other!'

Discussion: at the end of the activity, when both groups have finished, use, as appropriate, the following questions to promote discussion: 'How did you manage to share the pencils without speaking? What did you need to do?' Encourage responses such as: 'looked at what another person needed'(awareness of others), 'pointed at the pencil I wanted' (gesture), and 'nodded or shook my head' (gesture/affirmation).

5 and 6. Role-play and group discussion (20–30 minutes)

Group organization: students are arranged in pairs.

Remind students what is meant by role-play (drama). Explain that in this session we will be doing a role-play about listening and turn-taking skills, similar to the role-play in the last session. Organize students into pairs (A and B), giving A the role of speaker and B the role of listener. The scenario is about bad listening. Tell students:

A is going to tell B about his or her trip to the cinema (or something that he/she has done recently) and B is not going to listen properly. B is going to show bad listening by, for example, fidgeting, looking away or walking about the room.'

Allow five minutes for pairs to practise role-playing bad listening. Ask pairs to volunteer to show their role-plays to the rest of the group, giving one or two minutes per pair. Give time for discussion, asking students what they notice in each role-play and how the actors feel. Help students to make the connection between the listener's behaviour (rude, looks bored, etc.) and how the speaker is feeling (upset, cross, annoyed). How is the listener feeling?

PICTURES FOR COLOURING ACTIVITY

With students still organized in pairs say:

'For this role-play we will stay in our pairs. Each person will talk about their favourite food to their partner. However, rather than taking turns at speaking, everyone is going to talk at the same time.'

The two Leaders can give an example of this by each simultaneously telling the other about their favourite food. When this has been demonstrated, allow students two minutes to experience talking to each other at the same time. Then allow time for discussion. Ask students the following questions:

○ What did it feel like?

○ What did your partner tell you?

○ Was it easy or hard listening to them?

○ Was your partner listening to you?

○ If not, how did this make you feel?

Ask one or two pairs to demonstrate good listening and turn-taking to the group. Start with the two Leaders giving a demonstration. Choose a popular topic to discuss. After these role-plays ask the group what they noticed. Use the following questions to prompt discussion:

○ Did you notice good listening skills?

○ How did you know that people were taking turns in conversation?

○ Did both people like talking to each other?

○ If yes, why do you think this was?

7. Closing activity (5–8 minutes)

ACTIVITY: CHAIN LINKS

Materials: none
Group organization: students and group leaders seated on chairs arranged in a circle

Build a link – each student places their right arm in front of them and across their body. They place their left arm behind them, across their body to the right. With their right hand they, in turn, each take hold of the left hand of the person sitting next to them and keep holding. The chain will be complete when everyone has both hands held.

8. Compliments (5 minutes)

With students still sitting in a circle, but arms no longer linked, ask them to give a compliment about the person sitting on their left – something that person has done well in the session or more generally in school. This might include, for example, 'giving good answers', 'joining in role-play', 'sitting still', 'sharing pencils in class'. As compliments are given, record them on the pupil sheets (see Session 1).

9. Homework (5 minutes)

Good Listening Prompt Sheet from session 1 – share this sheet with someone in your family or with a friend at school. Point to those who are listening well. How do you know?

10. End session

Thank and congratulate students for completing the session.

✔

Model letter to parents/carers at the end of Session 2: Listening and turn-taking

Date:

Dear Parents/Carers,

This week our group learnt about listening and turn-taking. We reviewed some of the skills that help good listening, such as sitting or standing still, looking at the speaker and listening quietly (i.e. no talking) until the speaker has finished. The group enjoyed playing a turn-taking game. Students were each given a pattern and asked to colour it in a particular way. They were provided with one pot of pencils to share, and the pot contained just one of each colour needed for the design. The challenge was for everyone to complete their design in as fast a time as possible, sharing the pencils without speaking!

So how do you share and turn-take if you are not allowed to speak and to ask for things? Students learnt that by paying close attention to each other and looking for signs such as a nod or a gesture, it is possible to share and take-turns. Some students even started to anticipate the needs of others!

In our role-play we acted two scenarios, first with bad listening and turn-taking, and second, we discussed how a role-play with good listening and turn-taking might work out. Students volunteered to model this for the group. We discovered that conversations are best when people pay attention to each other and wait their turn to speak.

For homework this week students have again been given the Good Listening Prompt sheet to take home. They are asked once again to point to those who are listening well.

Over the week, take care to point out and praise any examples of good listening and turn-taking that your child shows.

Thanks for your help with the programme. Your support will make a difference.
Best wishes,

Names of Course Leaders

------------------------------✂------------------------------

Dear Parents/Carers, please complete this section and return it with your child when he/she attends the next session.
How did your child manage the homework?

How would you now rate his/her listening and turn-taking skills at home?

☐ Has a lot of difficulty ☐ Has some difficulty ☐ Has a little difficulty ☐ No difficulty

Session 3

Target area: Monitoring own body language and reading body language in others (Skill Area 3)

Session aims and preparation

Key learning aims

Students: Develop a concept of what body language is

Describe body language and facial expressions shown by others

Start to link body language with feelings

Understand why they need to pay attention to their own body language

Start to monitor their own body language

General aims

Students: Show increased sensitivity to others by paying more attention to the signals, given by others, that show how they feel

Show greater awareness of their own physical presentation, in particular body language, and of the messages that this sends to others (e.g. looking at the speaker generally shows attentiveness)

Link area of PSHE and Citizenship Curriculum

To build effective relationships through being able to recognize feelings in others, by improving ability to read body language. To develop independence and responsibility by monitoring own body language, the behaviour this shows and how this affects others.

Materials needed

Facial expressions cards, object cards (cut out individual cards), photos

Suggested additional materials

Hats and scarves, bag or basket and a few grocery items (e.g. packet of biscuits and a can of beans) for role-play

Session plan

1. Welcome to the group and warm-up activity (5–8 minutes)

ACTIVITY: PAIRS GAME (SIMILARITY BETWEEN TWO PERSONS)

Materials: none

Group organization: students and Group Leaders are seated on chairs arranged in a circle

Tell students that some of us have blonde hair and some brown. Some of us are tall and some small. Some of us have black shoes and some have brown. We do not look exactly the same as each other but we may look the same in some ways. This game is about noticing the ways in which we are the same as other people. Give an example of this, e.g. 'I have the same colour hair as Billy.' Ask each student to think of a way in which they look like someone else in the group. An example might be, 'I look like Taj as we both have red socks on.' or 'I look like Jenny as we both have blonde hair.' Tell students not to discuss what they have noticed with anyone else. They must wait for the group to guess when it is their turn. A Group Leader should start the activity by completing the following sentence: 'I look like (name of person).' The rest of the group must then guess at what they have in common. Allow five or six guesses before giving the answer, if necessary. Ensure everyone in the group has an opportunity to have a turn.

2. Recap on the previous session and on any homework set (5 minutes)

Use the following questions to help prompt discussion (if sessions are being followed in sequence):

- What did we learn last session?

- What is good listening?

- What is good turn-taking?

- Who practised good listening and turn-taking over the week?

- What happened when you showed good listening?

- What happened when you showed good turn-taking?

- Who noticed your good listening and turn-taking?

3. Introduction to this week's topic: body language (5–8 minutes)

Ask students: 'How do we let other people know what we are thinking?' Encourage students to think about how they might let a friend know they were feeling tired, bored, happy, etc. Help them to consider the different ways in which we let others know how we feel. Explain that, as well as telling someone how we are feeling, we can also show them by the way we look, i.e. by the way we are sitting or standing and what our faces our doing – perhaps smiling or frowning. This is 'body language'. So we can tell someone about the way we feel both by talking and by our body language.

4. Topic-linked activities (10 minutes)

There may not be time to play all four games so decide before the session which is most suitable for your group.

ACTIVITIES: READING FEELINGS

Materials: tape recorder, facial expressions cards, object cards, photos
Group organization: students are seated in a circle

1. Ask each student to give a word that describes a feeling (e.g. happy, angry, worried, bored, etc.). Tape the students' responses and play these back to them when everyone has had an opportunity to give a feeling word. Count together the number of responses given.

2. Show students the individual facial expressions cards, illustrating a range of facial expressions. Hold the cards up to the group and ask students to guess the emotion linked to each expression.

3. Deal the expression cards out to students, one card each face down. Ask each student to try to imitate or act their expression to the rest of the group. The group then guess what it might be.

4. Place cut-out object cards in the centre of the group, so that all students are able to see them. Ask students to try to match each facial expression card with a picture of an object (e.g. matching a 'frightened' expression with a picture of a spider). Encourage students to discuss their responses with each other and to work co-operatively in selecting pictures.

5 and 6. Role-play/drama and group discussion (25–30 minutes)

To reinforce the concept of body language, it is helpful if one of the two Leaders can role-model different feelings through body language. Give obvious examples of using body language to communicate different feelings, such as excited, worried or bored. When role-modelling different feelings, try not to speak but to demonstrate the emotion through facial expression, body posture and gestures. Ask students to guess how you might be feeling after each short role-play. As they make guesses, ask them how they know you are feeling tired, angry, happy, etc. Explain that they are able to guess how you feel as they are looking at your body language.

*   Ask students to watch the following drama carefully. They must focus on the characters' body language, i.e. what the characters are doing with their arms, legs, body and face. Students are told that the scene is set in a shop. Their task is to try and work out what is happening in the shop. Explain that they will have to work out the story from what the characters are

doing as they will not be saying anything. Students may be given the facial expressions cards to help focus their attention.

- Ideally, the role-play will be led by the two Group Leaders. One acts as a customer and the other as the shopkeeper. The scene starts happily, with the shopkeeper arranging the shelves and the customer putting items into a basket (both happy). The customer then goes to pay for her shopping but cannot find her purse (customer worried). She looks for it in her bag and on the floor (customer upset). The shopkeeper helps her look for it (shopkeeper puzzled). The customer then looks in her coat pocket and finds it there (customer and shopkeeper very happy, relieved). The customer pays for her goods and the shopkeeper puts them in a bag for her. The customer leaves the shop and waves at the shopkeeper as she does so. The shopkeeper waves back and smiles.

- At various points during the role-play it is helpful to freeze, asking students what they see. How does the shopkeeper look? Is the customer happy or worried? How do you know that?

GROUP DISCUSSION (10 MINUTES)

At the end of the role-play ask students to say what they thought had happened in the shop. Review the story. Ask:

- How did the customer feel when she was putting things in her basket?

- How did she feel when she had could not find her wallet?

- How did you know she was worried?

- When she was worried what did her face look like?

- Was she smiling then?

- Did the story end happily?

- How did they know that when no one said anything?

Help students to realize that they knew how both people felt as they were looking at their body language by asking: 'What did you see that tells you that she was worried?'

FACIAL EXPRESSIONS CARDS

OBJECT CARDS

7. Closing activities (8 minutes)

ACTIVITY: BUZZY BEES

Materials: none
Group organization: students are seated in a circle

Ask each student to say the sentence, 'The bees are buzzing', in a particular way. Use familiar emotions such as happy, excited, tired, sad, bored and scared. Ask other students to guess how each person is feeling as they are saying the sentence.

ACTIVITY: STORY CHAIN

Materials: none
Group organization: students are seated in a circle

For older or more able students, try telling a story in a particular way, e.g. as if you are all feeling very tired, i.e. in a slow voice, yawning, leaning back in chair. One of the Leaders starts the story and, in turn, each student adds a few words or sentences to create a group story. Remind students to say the story in the particular way chosen, e.g. tired.

8. Compliments (5 minutes)

With students still sitting in a circle, ask them to give a compliment about the person sitting on their left – something that person has done well in the session or more generally in school. This might include, for example, 'giving good answers', 'joining in role-play', 'sitting still', or 'sharing pencils in class'. When compliments are given, record them on the pupil sheets (see Session 1).

9. Homework (5 minutes)

Ask students to practise with family members to guess different facial expressions using prompt sheet symbols or photos – see Homework Sheets 3.1 and 3.2.

10. End session (5 minutes)

Ask the following question: 'How do we know that someone is happy/angry/sad, etc.?' Encourage students to recognize that we can see as well as hear how someone is feeling. Ask everyone to consider their own body language over the week and the signals it may give to other people. Thank and praise students for completing the session.

HOMEWORK SHEET 3.1: HOW DO THEY FEEL?

This week we learnt about body language. We can sometimes tell how someone feels by looking carefully at their body language. Look at the pictures below. Join each picture to a word that shows how the person feels.

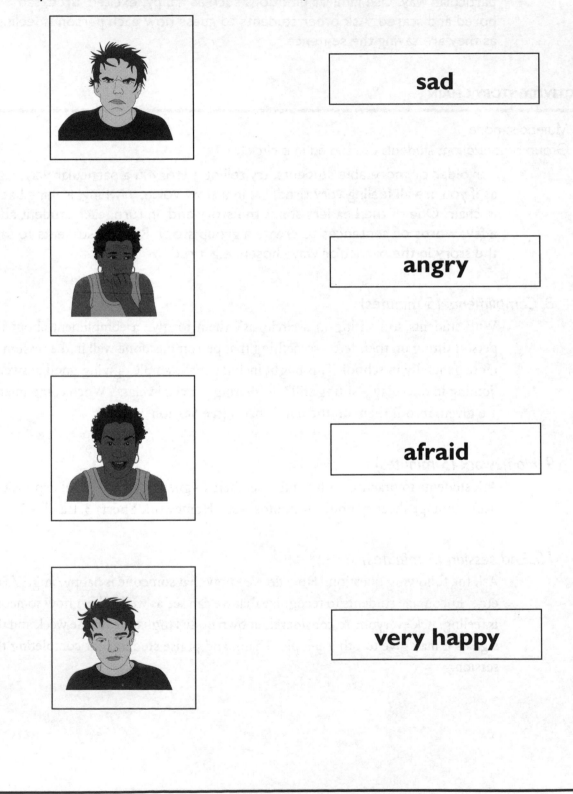

sad

angry

afraid

very happy

HOMEWORK SHEET 3.2: PICTURES OF FEELINGS

Look at the boxes below. The words in the boxes describe different feelings. Can you find pictures of people to match these feelings words? Look through old magazines and newspapers. Cut out pictures that match each word. Then stick them in the box next to the matching word if they fit. If not, keep hold of them and bring them to the next session.

Tired	Angry
Calm	Excited

Model letter to parents/carers at the end of Session 3: Monitoring and reading body language

Date:

Dear Parents/Carers,

Our social skills training this week focused on body language. We learnt that body language refers to the signals that we give others by the way we position our bodies and the facial expressions we make. We discovered that our body language could reveal our feelings. A person who is yawning, has his eyes closed and is slumped in his chair usually indicates that he is feeling bored or tired. In contrast, a person who is looking intently at the speaker and sitting upright in the chair gives the impression of being interested and alert.

Activities this week included recognizing different facial expressions and the emotions they portray. Our role-play was a real challenge as the actors were not allowed to speak. Students were asked to work out what was happening in the role-play and how the actors felt by paying close attention to their body language. They had to rely on visual clues alone. However, we discovered that we could tell a lot about how a person is feeling by reading their body language.

For homework students have been asked to match pictures of people showing different feelings with an appropriate feelings word. They have also been asked to look through old magazines and newspapers to find pictures of people showing particular feelings (tired, angry, calm and excited). Your child may need help with this activity. Please remind them to bring their pictures with them for the next session. You can reinforce your child's monitoring of their own body language by gently feeding back to them what you observe. Try to match expressions with a feeling, for example, 'You have put your head on the table – are you feeling tired?', or 'You have been smiling and laughing all the way home – it looks like you're very happy about something.'

Thanks again for your support with the programme. Have a good week.

Best wishes,

Names of Course Leaders

- ✂ -

Dear Parents/Carers, please complete this section and return it with your child when he/she attends the next session.
How did your child manage the homework?

Is your child paying:

☐ more attention to his/her body language   ☐ less attention   ☐ no different from before?

Session 4

Target area: Recognizing own and others' strengths (Skill Area 4)

Session aims and preparation

Key learning aims

Students: Identify and talk about their own strengths

           Identify a range of strengths in others

General aims

Students: Increase their self-confidence through recognizing their own strengths

           Value other people through recognition that everyone has their own set of skills

           Enjoy finding out more about themselves and others

Link area of PSHE and Citizenship Curriculum

Students make the most of their abilities by recognizing what they are good at. This will help them with setting simple targets for themselves. Students respect differences by recognizing worth in others and making positive statements about others. They show self-awareness by being able to express positive things about self and others.

Materials needed

Beanbag, cones (or other markers), Pupil Compliments Sheets

Suggested additional materials

Hats and scarves for role-play

Session plan

1. Welcome to the group and warm-up activity (8 minutes)

ACTIVITY: BRILLIANT BEANBAG

Materials: beanbag

Group organization: students and Group Leaders are seated on chairs arranged in a circle

Participants pass a beanbag to the person sitting on their left, completing the sentence 'I like…' when they take hold of the beanbag. They pass the beanbag a second time around the circle, this time completing the sentence, 'I am good at…' Ensure everyone in the group has an opportunity to participate.

2. Recap on the previous session and on any homework set (8 minutes)

Ask students, 'What did we talk about last session?' If the previous session was Session 3, ask: 'Who can tell me what body language means?' Give two or three demonstrations of different feelings, asking students to guess by your body language what they are (e.g. bored, excited, worried). Ask students how they might show you they are listening. Remind them of the body language that a person shows when they are listening well, e.g. sitting or standing still, looking at the speaker, not talking at the same time. Ask if students would like to share their diaries:

- Did anyone show good listening?

- Did anyone show the right body language in class?

- Who noticed?

- What did they say?

Praise students for their efforts.

3. Introduction to this week's topic: recognizing own and others' strengths (10 minutes)

The Group Leaders can introduce this topic by telling students the following:

'We are all members of this school; some are boys and some girls. We have different family backgrounds and enjoy different things. In this class some people enjoy music and are good at singing; some are good at football; some like watching television; some like eating chips; some enjoy swimming. We like to play football with someone who enjoys it as much as we do. Now let's think about activities you are good at. Let's have a game where we all think about one thing that we like.'

Ask each student to say one thing they like to do. Record their answers on a flip chart. Notice how some people like the same things and some people like different things. Help students to be aware of this.

4. Topic-related activity to help students understand the concept of strengths within us (10 minutes)

ACTIVITY: TRICKY TRAVEL!

Materials: two markers, e.g. cones or buckets

Group organization: circle seating (note circle may need to be widened to ensure there is enough space for markers)

Students remain seated in a circle with two markers placed diagonally through the room, approximately 6 to 8 feet apart. Various volunteers are asked to travel from one marker to the next in different ways. These might include one person hopping, one bouncing, one going on all fours and one walking backwards. Ask the group to observe who managed this task the fastest. Encourage students to think about what impacted on the participants' success. Praise all students for having a go, even when the game was hard for them. This shows that they are able to keep trying even when things get difficult.

5. Role-play/drama (25–30 minutes)

Ask two students to volunteer to take part in the role-play. Their task is to present their strengths to the rest of the group. Ideally they should share their skills in conversation and describe what they do and why they enjoy it. The rest of the group is asked to observe. Observers are asked to listen and look carefully at the role-play, to retell what is involved and what the students are good at. Students should select something that they are good at and confident about. Alternatively Group Leaders can discuss the following scenarios with the volunteers. The volunteers then tell the group about these scenarios.

SCENARIO A

Student 1 pretends that he is good at looking after his pet dog, giving it some food, looking at it, playing with it and taking it for walks. Examples of statements that the student could make during his role-play are as follows:

'I have a big, brown dog. His name is Scruffy. I brush his coat every day. He wakes me up in the morning. I give him some water and something to eat. Mum and I take him to the park for a walk. He loves running around and is a bit wild. One day he nearly ran away but I called him and he came back and I put him on a lead. Scruffy was then safe. He never bites me or any other person.'

Group discussion following Scenario A: Leaders facilitate discussion to tease out Student 1's strengths. In this example these might include being caring, looking after the dog well and being attentive.

SCENARIO B

Student 2 pretends that he is good at taking the register to and from the school office. Examples of statements the student could make are as follows:

'I am in school in time and always remember to get the register. I bring it to class and give it to the teacher. She calls out students' names. When she finishes I get up quietly and take the register from our class to the office. I put it in the right place. Sometimes, if I have time, I help the teacher to sharpen pencils and to put the chairs straight. She likes me to help her. I enjoy helping out in school.'

Group discussion following Scenario B: Leaders should facilitate the group discussion, helping observers to tease out Student 2's strengths. In this example these might include being reliable, being on time, being independent, and the fact that he knows his way around school and has a good memory for his job. Student B also notices when the pencils need sharpening and helps the teacher in general. He is able to follow a routine and enjoys his responsibilities. He can be trusted.

6. Group discussion: how do you know you are good at something? (10 minutes)

Encourage students to think about how they know they are good at something. Ask them to describe signs that tell them that they can do an activity well. Record their responses on a flip chart. Aim to include the following signs in discussion:

- The teacher or your parents say that you are good at something
- Your friends tell you that you are good at it
- You finish a task by yourself
- You like showing someone else how to do the task
- You get a reward for doing the activity well
- Other people ask you to carry out a task that you are good at
- You really enjoy the job and it makes you feel good

7. Closing activity (8 minutes)

ACTIVITY: SKILL SEARCH

Materials: flip chart and marker
Group organization: students sit in pairs around a circle

Ask students in pairs to spend three minutes finding out from each other what their partner is good at. Their task is then to act out or tell the whole group what they have found out about their partner. Record their responses on a flip chart. If a student has had difficulty selecting his or her own strengths, provide the necessary prompts and cues. Refer to their performance in previous sessions, e.g. 'I've noticed that you're really good at waiting your turn in the group.' It is important that every member of the group identifies something they are good at.

8. Compliments (5 minutes)

With students still sitting in a circle, ask them to give a compliment about the person sitting on their left – something that person has done well in the session or more generally in school. This might include, for example, 'giving good answers', 'joining in role-play', 'sitting still', or 'sharing pencils in class'. When compliments are given, record them on the pupil sheets (see Session 1).

9. Homework (5 minutes)

Ask students to complete Homework Sheet 4.1 (Skills and Strengths) for themselves and for three other people. These could be family members, friends at school or at home.

10. End session

Remind students that they all have special skills and strengths. Thank and praise students for completing the session.

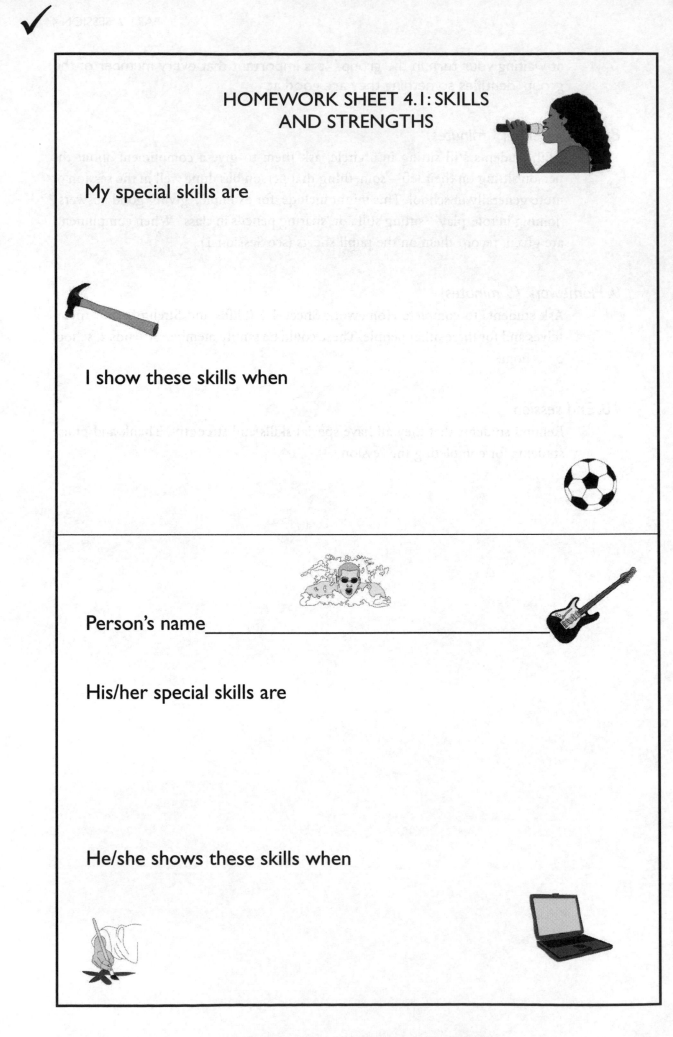

HOMEWORK SHEET 4.1: SKILLS AND STRENGTHS

My special skills are

I show these skills when

Person's name_____

His/her special skills are

He/she shows these skills when

Model letter to parents/carers at the end of Session 4: Recognizing strengths in ourselves and others

Date:

Dear Parents/Carers,

Our focus this week was to understand that we are all good at something. We each have individual strengths, which we may or may not share with our friends. Often the things that we are interested in are also our strengths, for example a skilled football player may especially enjoy watching football games on TV.

As a group we discussed how you know that you are good at something. Indicators included: being told so by another person such as a teacher or a parent; finishing a task by yourself; showing someone else how to do the task; getting high marks or a reward for a good job done; and enjoying the task. Students were asked to find out what their class-mates were good at as well as describe their own strengths and skills.

Identifying and acknowledging our own strengths are crucial for development of self-esteem. To ensure we have a positive self-image it is important to recognize not only our difficulties but also our skills. For homework this week students have been asked to write about or draw their special skills and to indicate when they show these skills. An example might be: 'My special skills are helping other people and being kind. I show these skills when I tidy the classroom and chat to my friends'. Special skills can be social (e.g. listens well to others), academic (e.g. good at spelling), physical (e.g. fast runner), emotional (e.g. caring towards friends) and practical (e.g. good at sewing). Please help your child to identify their own special skills and then write about or draw another person's skills, using the Homework Sheet 4.1: Skills and Strengths.

Again, thank you for your help.

Best wishes,

Names of Course Leaders

- - - - - - - - - - - ✂ -

Dear Parents/Carers, please complete this section and return it with your child when he/she attends the next session.
How did your child manage the homework?

How would you now rate your child's awareness of his/her strengths?

☐ Not at all aware   ☐ Somewhat aware   ☐ A good awareness   ☐ Clear about own skills

Please tick appropriate box.

Session 5

Target area: Learning to say no to unreasonable demands and to cope with peer pressure (Skill Area 5)

Session aims and preparation

Key learning aims

Students: Distinguish between reasonable and unreasonable requests

Are able to choose whether or not to agree to a request

Develop effective and confident ways to accept or reject demands made by others

General aims

Students: Are able to behave assertively when with other people

Are less likely to get into difficult or dangerous situations through peer pressure

Link area of PSHE and Citizenship Curriculum

Students develop independence and responsibility through being confident with new people and situations. They are able to respond assertively to others.

Suggested materials

Hats and scarves for role-play

Session plan

1. Welcome to the group and warm-up activity (5–8 minutes)

The following activity allows students to practise 'good-looking', co-operative game-playing and assertiveness skills.

ACTIVITY: COME INTO MY CHAIR

Materials: enough chairs for the game (half the number of chairs as game participants)

Group organization: chairs arranged in a circle with space for a person to pass between each chair.

Organize students so that half the group are seated in a circle on chairs. Each of the remaining students stands behind someone who is seated, except one person who stands behind an empty chair. The aim is for the person standing behind the empty chair to try to get someone seated to move to their chair by winking at them. People standing behind chairs must try to stop their seated partner from moving to the empty chair, by tapping them on the shoulder if they believe their partner has been winked at and is about to move. The aim is for all people standing to keep someone seated in the chair in front of them for as long as possible. Switch around 'standers' and 'sitters' after a few minutes.

DISCUSSION FOLLOWING ACTIVITY:

What did the person with the empty chair have to do?

How did he or she do this?

Which special skills were needed?

Encourage responses that emphasize the importance of looking and paying attention.

2. Recap on the previous session and on any homework set (8 minutes)

If the previous session was Session 4, ask students: 'What did we talk about last week?' Use prompts to help them recall the main topic – that we all have strengths. Ask: 'How do you know what your strengths are? How do you know you are good at something?' Encourage students to recall the following:

- The teacher or your parents say that you are good at something

- Your friends tell you that you are good at it

- You finish a task by yourself

- You like showing someone else how to do the task

- You get a reward for doing the activity well

- Other people ask you to carry out a task that you are good at

- You really enjoy the job and it makes you feel good

Ask students how their homework went. Who recorded their own strengths or special skills? Who found out about another person's special skills? What were these? Did any students discover new special skills over the week? Who in their family or peers noticed their special skills?

3. Introduction to this week's topic: learning to say no when friends want you to do something that you don't want to do (10 minutes)

Discussion: ask students to give examples of the different things their friends might ask them to do. Record responses in one of two columns on the board: good or bad. (The terms 'helpful' and 'unhelpful' can be used instead if students are familiar with these.) Ask students to try not to give names of people, e.g. rather than saying 'Kate told me to throw the rubber', the student should try to say 'someone/a friend/a classmate told me to throw the rubber'.

Examples of good (helpful) suggestions and bad (unhelpful) suggestions are as follows:

Good / Helpful	Bad / Unhelpful
My friends ask me to play football with them.	My friends tell me to take sweets without paying for them.
A friend asks me to help tidy the class.	My classmate tells me to hide the teacher's pen.
My classmates tell me I should do my homework.	A boy tells me to miss the lesson.
A boy in my class said 'Let's tidy our desks'.	A girl at school said I want you to be my best friend and you are not allowed any other friends.
A girl told me to tie my shoelace otherwise I might trip over.	An older boy said 'I dare you to smash the fire alarm'.

Ask students: 'What would happen if you went along with a good suggestion?' (Give an example, such as, 'A friend asks me to join his game at playtime.') Encourage positive responses such as: 'I'd not feel left out', 'I'd have a fun time', etc.

Now ask students: 'What would happen if you went along with a bad suggestion?' (Give an example, such as, 'My friends tell me to steal some chocolate'.) Encourage responses that identify the trouble or problems that result from going along with bad suggestions. Examples might be: 'I'd get into trouble', 'I'd feel bad', or 'My mum would get upset'.

4. Topic game (10 minutes)

ACTIVITY: SUGGESTIONS

Materials: sheet with quiz questions
Group organization: students to sit in pairs

Ask students to listen carefully to the following sentences. Say: 'Which ones are good suggestions and which are bad?' Ask different pairs to share their ideas after each sentence has been read out. This can be used to generate further discussion within the group.

SUGGESTIONS

1. Hey, let's work quietly, then we can get our work finished.
2. You've got to take that book. You won't be my friend otherwise.
3. Come on; let's miss the next lesson, no one will notice.
4. Let's ask that boy to play as he looks lonely.
5. Give me your crisps or I'll hit you.
6. Let's tidy the class and then our teacher will be pleased.
7. If you hit that boy, then I'll give you some sweets.
8. You look hungry. Have one of my sandwiches.

HARDER SUGGESTIONS

1. Let's be best friends and always sit together.
2. I forgot my lunch today. Please can I have half your sandwich?
3. I get really scared at break because I always get teased. I don't wan't to go to the playground. Please will you hide in the class with me?
4. Let's not ask her to join our game because she always bosses us about.

5. Role-play/drama (25–30 minutes)

Explain to students that it is important to learn how not be pushed into doing things that we do not want to do. It is much easier to say 'yes' than 'no'. Saying 'no' is sometimes the brave thing to do. There are some good ways of saying 'no'. When a person asks us to do something and we don't want to, we can just tell them politely but straight out: 'No thanks, I don't want to.' We will now role-play this.

Ideally Leaders should give an example role-play, illustrating how to say 'no' to an unwanted demand. The following script may be used with each of the Leaders taking a role.

A: 'I've a great idea; let's hide our pencils. Then we won't have to write anything.'

B: 'No thanks, I don't want to do that.'

A: 'Come on, it will be funny.'

B: 'No thanks, I don't want to.'

A: 'You're a real scaredy cat.'

B: 'No thanks, I don't want to.'

A: 'Oh, OK then.'

In pairs ask students to role-play the above scenario (or similar scenarios of their choice), to practise saying 'no' to bad suggestions. Remind the Bs to use the direct approach, saying 'No thanks, I don't want to'. Give an opportunity for pairs to volunteer to show their role-play to the rest of the group.

Discussion: ask students why it can be difficult to say 'no'. What might another person say to try to get you to say 'yes'? Give examples such as:

'I won't be your friend unless you do it.'

'You're stupid if you don't do it.'

'You're a baby if you don't do it.'

'It'll be really fun.'

Tell students that if they still manage to say 'no' when another person is really trying to push them to do something bad, they are being very strong.

6. Group discussion (10 minutes)

Ask students if they can think of a time when a friend has told them to do something that they did not want to take part in. What happened? Did they manage to say 'no' or did they go along with it? If they said 'yes', did they have to? What is the worst thing that could have happened if they said 'no'? How does it feel to say 'no'? What is the worse thing that could have happened by going along with their friend's suggestion?

Tell students that when other people are pushing us to do things it can be hard to say 'no'. We want to please other people and worry that they won't be our friends if we don't say 'yes' to them. A good friend will not stop being your friend if you stick with your beliefs. If someone is being a good friend, then they will respect you for doing what you think is best.

7. Closing activity (5–8 minutes)

ACTIVITY: BEANBAG GAME 2

Materials: beanbag
Group organization: students standing in a circle

> Follow instructions for beanbag game 1 (Session 1). However, this time, as a participant throws the beanbag to another person, they say his or her name rather than their own. Aim to increase the speed of throwing and catching if possible. Slow down gradually towards the end.

8. Compliments (5 minutes)

> With students still sitting in a circle, ask them to give a compliment about the person sitting on their left – something that person has done well in the session or more generally in school. This might include, for example, 'giving good answers', 'joining in role-play', 'sitting still', or 'sharing pencils in class'. When compliments have been given, record them on the pupil sheets.

9. Homework (5 minutes)

> Ask students to draw or write about occasions when a peer has asked or told them to do something. Students can make a daily record or focus on just one or two days during the course of the week (Homework Sheet 5.1: Do I have to do what they say?). Students should try to categorize the request as either good/helpful or bad/unhelpful. If possible they should also document their response.

10. End session

> Praise and congratulate students for completing the session. They are now half way through the programme! Remind students that they often have the power to make their own decisions.

HOMEWORK SHEET 5.1: DO I HAVE TO DO WHAT THEY SAY?

	Good (helpful) or bad (unhelpful) suggestion	What I did	Good or bad suggestion?
Monday	Example: An older boy told me to get his lunch.	Example: I said no because that's not my job.	Good or Bad
Tuesday			Good or Bad
Wednesday	Example: My sister asked me to help her wash up.	Example: I helped her and we did it really fast. Mum was happy.	Good or Bad
Thursday			Good or Bad
Friday			Good or Bad

Model letter to parents/carers at the end of Session 5: Learning to say no to unreasonable demands

Date:

Dear Parents/Carers,

We started our topic work this week by discussing the types of things that other people, such as classmates, might ask us to do. We decided whether each suggestion was either a good/helpful one or a bad/unhelpful one. An example of a good suggestion might be 'A friend asks me to join in a game of football at break'. In contrast a bad suggestion might be 'A boy tells me to miss the lesson and play on the computer instead'.

Students then thought about the consequences of going along with a good or a bad suggestion. They discussed how going along with a bad suggestion often leads to unhappy feelings, for example the consequences of missing a lesson to play on the computer might be extra homework or shorter breaks. In addition important information given during the lesson would be missed. Students talked about the benefits of going along with a good suggestion, for example joining in a football game at break could be fun and friendship building.

In role play we learnt how to avoid being pushed into something we don't want to do. Students practiced the direct approach of saying 'no' or 'no thanks' clearly and firmly. They discovered that even when faced with persistence this approach works well. We talked about how it's often easier to say 'yes' than 'no' to a friend, as we don't want to upset them or lose them as a friend. But we also learnt that it is more important to do what we believe is right.

For homework your child has been asked to draw or write about occasions when a peer asks them to do something at school. He or she can choose to make a daily record or focus on just one or two days during the week. Help your child to decide whether the request is a good/helpful one or a bad/unhelpful one. Encourage them to write or draw their response. If your child has difficulty finding examples from school, help him or her use home situations, e.g. requests made by siblings. Good luck with the homework!
Best wishes,

Names of Course Leaders

- - - - - - - - - - - - - - - - - - ✂ -

Dear Parents/Carers, please complete this section and return it with your child when he/she attends the next session.
How did your child manage the homework?

How would you now rate your child's awareness of his/her strengths?

☐ Not at all aware   ☐ Somewhat aware   ☐ A good awareness   ☐ Clear about own skills

Please tick appropriate box.

85

Session 6

Target area: Recognizing and describing feelings (Skill Area 6)

Session aims and preparation

Key learning aims

Students: Expand their vocabulary for describing a range of feelings

Become better at reading a person's facial expressions and body language to determine broadly how they are feeling (happy, sad, worried, angry, excited, bored, pleased)

Understand that we usually experience lots of different feelings each day

General aims

Students: Empathize more readily with peers by being able to detect with greater sensitivity how they are feeling

Express their own feelings more effectively, enhancing opportunities for appropriate support from others

Are better able to move forward from unhappy or angry feelings by understanding that we experience a range of feelings and emotions every day

Link area of PSHE and Citizenship Curriculum

Students recognize and name feelings, and they are able to express positive things about self and others. Students recognize feelings in different situations. They start to manage emotions more effectively. Students express their feelings and recognize the impact they have on others.

Materials needed

Facial expressions cards

Suggested additional materials

Hats and scarves for role-play

Session plan

1. Welcome to the group and warm-up activity (10 minutes)

ACTIVITY: CHANGE THE ACTION

Materials: none
Group organisation: students and Group Leaders seated on chairs arranged in a circle

One student volunteers to be, or is designated, the Detective. He/she is asked to leave the room (or stand away from the group) whilst a Guide is being chosen. From the remainder of the group a student is designated the Guide and the rest become the Followers. The Guide's job is to initiate actions such as tapping own knees, tapping own shoulders, clapping hands and tapping feet on the ground. The Followers follow the Guide's actions. For example, the Guide might start by clapping his/her hands. The Followers copy this action. Thirty seconds later the Guide changes the action to standing up and sitting back down in his/her seat. Again the Followers follow this action until the Guide decides to change to a new action.

Once the Guide has been chosen, the Detective returns to the group, unaware of whom the Guide is. The Detective's job is to determine who is leading the activities (i.e. the Guide) by looking carefully as the group carry out and change actions. As students become more familiar with this game, the Guide and Followers will learn to become more subtle in their actions. This might include Followers looking mostly at someone other than the Guide (so as not to give away the Guide!) and the Guide changing the action when the Detective is looking at someone else.

If possible, allow all students the chance of being either the Guide or the Detective. At the end of the game, briefly discuss the skills needed. These include looking carefully, paying attention and facing each other.

2. Recap on the previous session and on any homework set (8 minutes)

The group remains seated in a circle. Remind students that last session (if Session 5) we learnt about how to 'say no' when other people tell us to do things that are bad or unhelpful. Ask for volunteers to feed back from their homework diaries. How did students cope with bad suggestions? Did anyone manage to 'say no'? What happened when they did this? How did they feel? Remind students that if someone is being a good friend then they will not tell you to do something bad or dangerous. Getting someone into trouble is not a friendly thing to do. A good friend will let you make good choices.

3. Introduction to this week's topic: looking at feelings (10 minutes)

Discussion: tell students that sometimes we are happy and sometimes sad. We feel lots of other things too, such as excited, bored or lonely. Ask students to volunteer to tell the group about a time they have felt happy. If appropriate, try to expand on the students' use of adverbs when asking them about their experience. An example of this might be as follows. A student volunteers: 'I was very happy on Saturday, as it was my birthday. I was very happy about opening my presents. I got a football and I was very happy.' The Leader responds: 'Lucky you getting such a good present. You were happy when you saw your presents. Were you also excited?' Encourage students to think about the range of feelings they have experienced.

4. Topic-related activity (10 minutes)

ACTIVITY: WHAT'S THE FEELING?

Materials: facial expressions cards, board and marker for recording students' responses
Group organization: students seated on chairs in a semicircle. Ensure students can clearly see the board from where they are sitting

Show students cards depicting people showing different feelings. Hold one card up at a time and ask students how each person is feeling. Record their responses as a list on the board – in writing if students are able to read, or as simple facial expressions if they cannot read. When all cards have been shown, ask students to choose one of the feelings from the list and not tell anyone their choice (whisper a feelings word to the student if they are unsure of which one to choose). In turn ask each student to walk about the room in a way that shows the feeling they have chosen. It may be helpful for Leaders to give an example of this, e.g. to walk about the room looking grumpy or excited. After each student has role-played a different emotion, ask other students to guess what it might be.

5. Role-play/drama (25–30 minutes)

Students sit in a semicircle facing the Leaders. Ideally the Group Leaders should take the role of Actors for this role-play as different emotions need to be clearly and accurately depicted. The facial expressions cards are laid out in front of the students, either placed on the floor or on a table in the middle of the group. The Actors role-play a conversation between friends. They show a range of emotions and expressions throughout their conversation, starting with excitement/happiness at seeing each other.

After about a minute they freeze the role-play. A student is then asked to select a facial expression card that shows how the Actors feel. Actors then continue with the role-play, freezing at various intervals and asking a different student each time to select a card that shows how one or both of the Leaders feel at that point.

Leaders should ask students about the different expressions, such as: 'Why does the Actor look sad? What has happened to make him/her feel like that?' Remind students to look out for clues to help them work out how the Actors are feeling during the role-play. 'Are they smiling or frowning? Are their voices happy or sad? What does their body language tell you?'

POSSIBLE SCRIPT FOR LEADERS: 'WHAT'S THE FEELING' ROLE-PLAY. THE SCRIPT MAY BE MIMED ONCE IT HAS BEEN PLAYED WITH WORDS

Leader A: Hello, what a nice surprise to see you. (happy / surprised)

Leader B: Yes, it's good to see you too. (happy / surprised)

Leader A: We haven't seen each other for a long time. (happy)

Leader B: Well I suppose we've both been busy. (happy)

FREEZE. Ask students how Leaders are feeling? How do they know (smiling, happy voice)?

Leader A: Are you still working in the shop? (happy)

Leader B: Yes, but something awful happened last week. (sad)

Leader A: Oh no, what was that? (worried)

Leader B: We had a burglary in the shop and all the money in the till was stolen. (upset)

Leader A: How terrible. I hope nobody got hurt by the burglars. (worried)

FREEZE. Ask students how Leaders are feeling? How do they know? Leader A – worried, anxious, concerned, upset. Leader B – upset, sad.

Leader B: Well at least nobody was hurt. (calm / relieved)

Leader A: That's a good thing. (pleased)

Leader B: We're pleased as the police have caught the burglars. (pleased)

Leader A: Yes, that's good. (calm)

FREEZE. Ask students how Leaders are feeling? How do they know?

Leader B: Well I've told you what happened to me. How are you? (question)

Leader A: I had a nice surprise as my dog has just had puppies! (happy)

Leader B: Oh that's good. How many puppies are there? (happy)

Leader A: Seven. If you are not in a hurry would you like to come and see them? (happy)

Leader B: Yes, I'd really love to. Shall we go now? (excited)

Leader A: Yes and I'll make some tea as well. (pleased)

Leader B: This has really turned out to be a happy day! (happy)

FREEZE. Ask students how Leaders are feeling? How do they know?

6. Group discussion (10–15 minutes)

Remind students that we can often find out how a person is feeling by asking them. Sometimes people like to talk about how they feel. What happens when you are feeling sad? Do you tell a friend or someone in your family? Does your friend tell you if he or she is feeling sad?

Sometimes people feel sad but don't tell you. How might you know they are unhappy? Encourage students to talk about non-verbal cues, such as frowning, crying, head in hands. Remind students that we can tell a lot about how someone is feeling by looking carefully at their body language and facial expressions.

7. Closing activity (8 minutes)

ACTIVITY: HAPPY ENDINGS!

Materials: none
Group organization: students and Leaders are seated on chairs arranged in a circle

Students complete the sentence 'I feel happy when …', using their own words. A Leader should start the game saying, 'We are going to take turns at finishing the sentence "I feel happy when…". I will go first to show you what I mean. "I feel happy when it's sunny outside" (or something more abstract if appropriate, such as "…when a student in my class learns something new")'. The person sitting to the Leader's left then has a go at completing the sentence. Continue around the group until all students have had an opportunity to respond. Encourage full participation but enable students to pass if they wish.

8. Compliments (5 minutes)

With students still sitting in a circle, ask them to give a compliment about the person sitting on their left – something that person has done well in the session or more generally in school. This might include, for example, 'giving good answers', 'joining in role-play', 'sitting still' or 'sharing pencils in class'. When compliments are given record them on the pupil sheets.

9. Homework (5 minutes)

Ask students to keep a diary of their feelings over the week. Students should try to record one or two feelings each day on Homework Sheet 6.1, either in writing or with a face drawing (e.g. a smiley, angry or grumpy face). If possible they should write or draw what made them feel that way. A completed example of Homework Sheet 6.1 is provided to help Leaders and students.

10. End session (3 minutes)

Praise and congratulate students for completing the session. Remind students that we all experience good and bad feelings. We have lots of different feelings each day. The more we know about feelings, the better we can deal with our own bad or unhappy feelings. We also get better at noticing how other people feel.

SAMPLE HOMEWORK SHEET: FEELINGS

Name: Kelly

Day	What was the feeling?	When did you feel that way?	What made you feel that way?
Monday	Very happy and excited	Morning Afternoon Evening	I did well in spelling and got them all right.
Tuesday	A bit annoyed	Morning Afternoon Evening	My sister borrowed my pink jeans and didn't tell me. I spent ages looking for them.
Wednesday	Nice and calm and relaxed	Morning Afternoon Evening	Mrs Johnson came to do yoga with our class. It was really nice and a bit hard with all the stretching. I felt good after it.
Thursday	Sad and crying a bit	Morning Afternoon Evening	I lost my special bracelet that my uncle gave me. Mum helped me look for it but we couldn't find it anywhere.
Friday	Happy	Morning Afternoon Evening	I visited Lisa my friend after school. Her mum gave us pizza and lemonade.

HOMEWORK SHEET 6.1: FEELINGS

Name:

Day	What was the feeling?	When did you feel that way?	What made you feel that way?
Monday		Morning Afternoon Evening	
Tuesday		Morning Afternoon Evening	
Wednesday		Morning Afternoon Evening	
Thursday		Morning Afternoon Evening	
Friday		Morning Afternoon Evening	

Model letter to parents/carers at the end of Session 6: Recognizing and describing feelings

Date:

Dear Parents/Carers

We started our topic this week with a discussion about the different feelings that we experience. Students learnt that they experience a range of feelings each day. They rarely feel just happy or just sad or just angry for a whole day. We talked about real examples of times that we have felt happy, excited, angry or other strong feelings. During role-play students were asked to detect the different feelings shown by the actors, by looking carefully at their facial expressions and body language. Students were also encouraged to listen to each actor's tone of voice and to use this information to help understand how the actor was feeling. They started to differentiate between happy, sad, worried and excited voices.

Students were asked what they did when they felt sad. Did they tell a friend or someone in their family? What happened next? Students talked about how they might know that someone is feeling sad. They learnt that facial expressions, such as a smile or frown, could show a lot about how someone feels. Body language and tone of voice (e.g. loud and angry) can also indicate a person's feelings.

Over the next week your child's homework involves keeping a diary of his or her feelings. If possible he or she should try to record one or two feelings each day, either in writing or with a face drawing (e.g. smiley, angry, grumpy, etc.). Encourage your child to write, draw or talk about what made them feel that way. Please use the homework sheet provided. Thanks for your support.

Best wishes,

Names of Course Leaders

·····················✂···

Dear Parents/Carers, please complete this section and return it with your child when he/she attends the next session.
How did your child manage the homework?

Can your child recognize any of these feelings in himself or herself? (Please circle)

Happy   Excited   Sad   Worried   Tired   Angry

Can your child recognize any of these feelings in others? (Please circle)

Happy   Excited   Sad   Worried   Tired   Angry

Session 7

Target area: Learning to control own feelings (Skill Area 7)

Session aims and preparation

Key learning aims

Students: Understand the concepts of public and private

Recognize which thoughts and feelings should be kept private and which can be shared in public

Start to understand the impact that words can have on other people

General aims

Students: Show greater sensitivity to others by understanding the impact of our words and actions on others

Have increased safety in the wider environment by not carrying out private acts in public

Respect other people's need for privacy

Link area of PSHE and Citizenship Curriculum

Students recognize the impact of their actions and words on others. They are able to put self in other's shoes and to show care for others

Materials needed

Set of public signs pictures, set of public places pictures, set of private places pictures, sorting hoops, public sentence tape (any commercially available tape would do), private/public places worksheet, feelings worksheet

Suggested additional materials

Hats and scarves for role-play

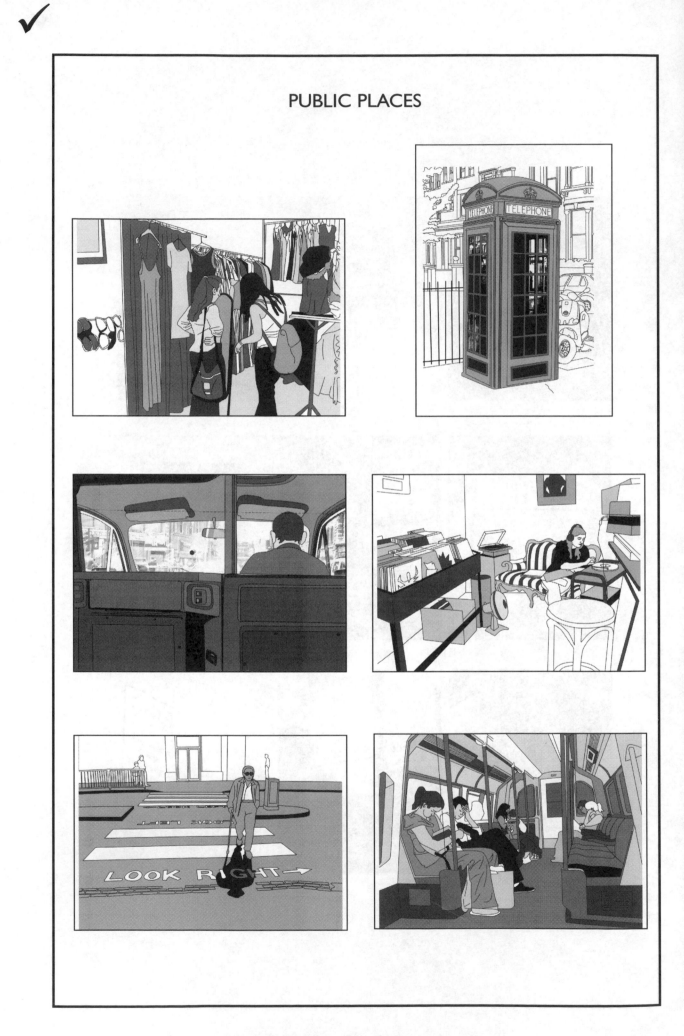

PRIVATE PLACES

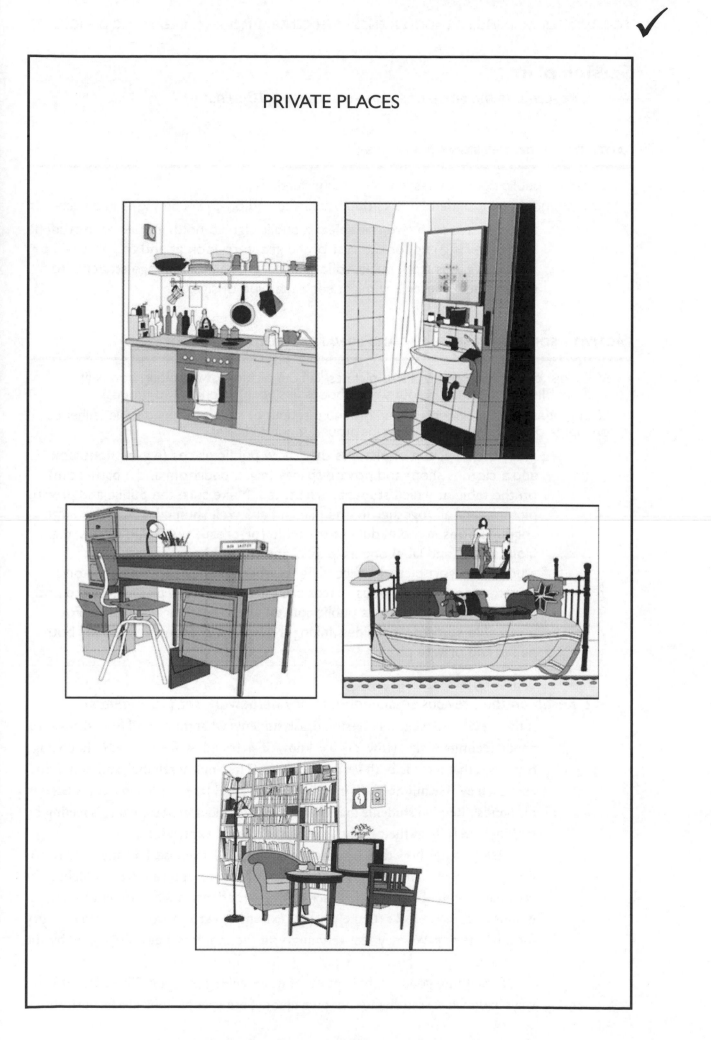

Session plan

1. Welcome to the group and warm-up activities (18 minutes)

ACTIVITY: GUESS THE SIGN (10 MINUTES)

Materials: public signs pictures (cut out each picture)

Group organization: students and Group Leaders seated on chairs arranged in a circle

> **Students are each given or select a public sign to hold. In turn each student holds their sign up for the rest of the group to look at and to guess what it means, e.g. bus stop, public toilets, underground. Encourage students to think about where they might see each type of sign.**

ACTIVITY: SORTING GAME (PUBLIC AND PRIVATE SPACES) (8 MINUTES)

Materials: public and private places pictures (cut out pictures), two sorting hoops (if students all work together) or four sorting hoops (if students work in two groups)

Group organization: students seated around a square or circular shaped table, either as one large group or two smaller groups around separate tables

> **Place the selection of pictures that show public places (e.g. a phone box and a clothes shop) and private spaces (e.g. a bedroom and a bathroom) on the table at which students are seated. Make sure the public and private pictures are all together in one pile and are well shuffled. Place two large sorting hoops in the middle of the table (or create two large circles, e.g. from string) and label one as 'public' and the other as 'private'. Ask students to sort pictures according to whether they show a public or a private space. If ambiguous spaces are introduced (e.g. places that are both public and private, such as public toilets) allow time for discussion. For more able students, consider linking the hoops, creating a space for both public and private places.**

2. Recap on the previous session and on any homework set (10 minutes)

If the previous session was Session 6, ask students what they recall from the session about feelings. Ask: 'How do we know if a friend is feeling sad?' Encourage responses that include both verbal cues, like, 'They might tell me', and non-verbal cues such as, 'He might be crying', 'He'd have a sad face', or 'He'd put his head in his hands'. Remind students that we can tell a lot about how someone is feeling by looking carefully at their body language and facial expressions.

Ask students how they managed the homework exercise. Did anyone write or draw the same feeling each day? Did anyone write or draw a different feeling for each day? Remind students that each day we experience many different feelings. It is unusual for us to feel extremely happy, extremely excited, extremely sad or angry for a whole day. We may feel very angry in the morning but quite happy by the afternoon.

Something good might happen for us to feel happy again. There are different ways in which we can change our own mood. Some people look at a favourite book or go for a quiet walk when they are angry. This makes them feel calm. Tell students we will talk more about how we can change our own moods in another session.

3. Introduction to this week's topic: public and private (10 minutes)

Tell students that in our warm-up games we were thinking about public and private places. Public means 'for everyone' and private means 'not for everyone'. Now give an example of something we might do in public, such as buying some food or reading a book. Tell students that when we are in the classroom we are in a public place. Ask for examples of the different things students do in class, e.g. writing, talking and reading. Next ask students if they do the following things in class: brush their teeth, wash their hair and change their underwear. Encourage students to think about why they might do these things in their bedroom or bathroom but not in the classroom. Use the terms 'public' and 'private'.

4. Topic-related activity (10 minutes)

ACTIVITY: LISTENING TO SENTENCES

Materials: sentence tape, public/private thoughts worksheet, feelings worksheet
Group organization: students should be seated at a desk or at a space where they can comfortably write

Give each student a copy of the public/private thoughts worksheet. Ask them to listen carefully to the list of related statements and to think about whether each statement can be said out loud or whether it should be kept as a private thought. Explain that private thoughts may sometimes be shared with someone they know very well, such as parents, but would not be shared, for example, with their whole class. Ask children to decide, as they listen to each sentence, whether to tick the thought bubble (private) or the speech bubble (public).

When students have completed the activity, discuss their choices. Encourage them to think about their reasons why some thoughts should be kept private. Ask: 'How would another person feel if you said the thought out loud?' 'How would you feel if someone said that thought to you?' As an extension activity, sentences may be read out loud again, this time with students focusing on how the listener might feel. Answers are then recorded using the feelings worksheet.

5 and 6. Role-play/drama and group discussion (25–30 minutes)

Arrange students into pairs (A and B). Ask A to tell B about his or her favourite TV programme. Ask B to respond by looking very bored, yawning and saying: 'This is boring.' Allow role-play to run for two to three minutes and then reassemble the group. Ask the As how their partner B made them feel. If B was bored, was it OK for him/her to let A know? Should B have kept this feeling private?

PRIVATE THOUGHT (WHAT I THINK)
AND PUBLIC THOUGHT (WHAT I SAY)

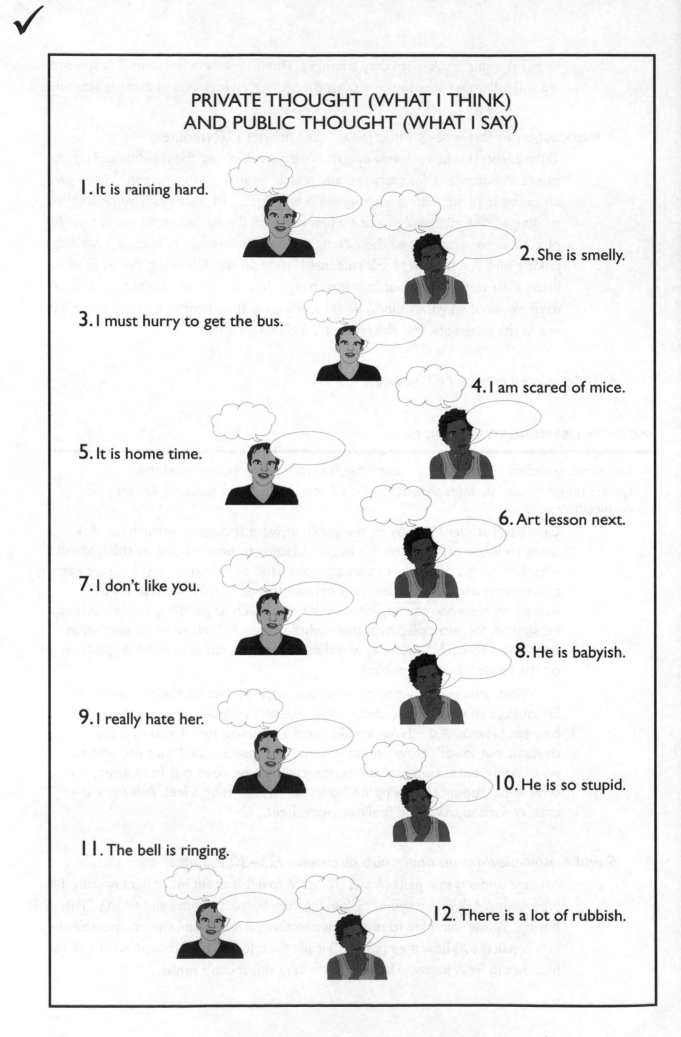

1. It is raining hard.

2. She is smelly.

3. I must hurry to get the bus.

4. I am scared of mice.

5. It is home time.

6. Art lesson next.

7. I don't like you.

8. He is babyish.

9. I really hate her.

10. He is so stupid.

11. The bell is ringing.

12. There is a lot of rubbish.

Now ask one pair to role-play A talking about a TV programme to B and B listening well. Discuss with students how A felt this time. Encourage responses such as: 'good about himself', 'happy because he is being listened to', 'important because his friend is listening to him'.

7. Closing activity (8 minutes)

ACTIVITY: CHANGING PLACES

Materials: none

Group organization: arrange chairs in a circle so that all students are seated except one, who stands on the outside of the circle. Ensure there is enough space between each chair so that students can easily pass between chairs.

A Leader calls out the names of two seated students who must swap seats, going around the outside of the circle in order to do so. The Leader uses the following phrase with the appropriate names: 'Jim and Susy ready, go!' The aim is for the student without a seat to reach and sit in one of the two empty seats as quickly as he/she can, before one of the moving students reaches it. Students must go clockwise around the circle and only go to a free seat when they are right behind it.

8. Compliments (5 minutes)

With students still sitting in a circle, ask them to give a compliment about the person sitting on their left – something that person has done well in the session or more generally in school. This might include, for example, 'giving good answers', 'joining in role-play', 'sitting still' or 'sharing pencils in class'. When compliments are given, record them on the pupil sheets.

9. Homework (5 minutes)

Ask students to keep a diary of all the public places they go to during the week (Homework Sheet 7.1). Encourage students to list some of the activities they engage in at each public place. When students have recorded the different public places they have attended, they should then consider if they could carry out a private activity (such as brushing teeth or changing clothes) in any of these places.

10. End session (2 minutes)

Praise and congratulate students for completing the session. Help students recognize the progress they are making with social skills.

✓

HOMEWORK SHEET 7.1: DIARY OF PUBLIC PLACES

Today's date:

Type of public place:

Activities I did there:

Could I do a private activity there like brush my teeth?

Yes   or   No

Model letter to parents/carers at the end of Session 7: Learning to control our own feelings

Date:

Dear Parents/Carers,

We started our topic this week by learning about the concepts of public and private. First we looked at and identified a range of public signs, for example the signs for a bus stop and a train station. Students then looked at pictures of different places and sorted them into one of two categories, public or private. A picture of a football stadium was considered a public place whereas a picture of a bedroom was thought to be private.

We discovered that public means 'for everyone' and private means 'not for everyone'. Students were asked to give examples of something they might do in a public place, such as the classroom. They were then challenged to give examples of things they might do in a private place such as the bathroom. We talked about why it is OK to carry out private things, such as getting dressed, in a private space but usually not a good idea in a public place. Students were reminded that most activities that relate to personal hygiene are private as we show parts of our bodies that are usually kept clothed in public.

Our topic extended to deciding when our thoughts should be kept private (i.e. to ourselves) and when they can be shared in public. Students heard different statements (e.g. 'He smells terrible' and 'You look great') and decided which of these statements could be shared in public (with others) and which should be kept private (to themselves). They role-played sharing thoughts in public and keeping them private.

For homework this week your child has been asked to keep a diary or record of any public place that they go to during the week. This could be, for example, a school, a local swimming pool or a park. Encourage your child to record, by writing or drawing, the activity they engage in whilst at the public place. Ask your child if he or she would carry out a private activity, such as brushing teeth and changing clothes, in any of these places.

Best wishes,

Names of Course Leaders

- - - - - - - - - - - - - - ✂ -

Dear Parents/Carers, please complete this section and return it with your child when he/she attends the next session.

How did your child manage the homework?

What is your child's understanding of public and private?

Session 8

Target area: Being confident to explain own views and to ask for support when needed (Skill Area 8)

Session aims and preparation

Key learning aims

Students: Are confident to share their views with others in a group setting

Recognize situations when help is needed from another person

Know when to ask for help

Know how to ask for help

General aims

Students: Enjoy participating in group discussions

Draw on surrounding resources when experiencing difficulty, both at school and in the wider environment

Link area of PSHE and Citizenship Curriculum

Students are able to ask questions and to talk with adults about thoughts and feelings. Students use different approaches to decision-making (e.g. asking for adult advice where appropriate).

Suggested materials

A marble, hats and scarves for role-play

Session plan

1. Welcome to the group and warm-up activity (10 minutes)

ACTIVITY: COMPLETE THAT SENTENCE (10 MINUTES)

Materials: none

Group organization: students and Group Leaders are seated on chairs arranged in a circle

Group Leaders start and students follow, completing the sentence, 'I like...', for example, 'I like sweets'. Encourage all students to participate in providing a response. In a similar manner, ask students to complete the sentence, 'I worry about...'. Finish the activity with, 'I feel happy when...'. Praise students for giving an answer. Tell them that it is good to join in when we are sharing our thoughts and feelings as a group.

2. Recap on the previous session and on any homework set (8 minutes)

If the previous meeting was Session 7, ask students what they remember from the session. Ask: 'Who can give an example of a public place?' Prompt students to refer to their homework diary. Ask: 'Who can name a private place?' 'What sorts of activities should you do only in a private place?' Remind students that the sorts of things we do in public and private can depend on a person's culture. Tell students that in Britain it is usual to carry out hygiene activities, such as bathing and dressing, in private. In other cultures it may be acceptable to bath in public. Remind students that our thoughts can also be public or private. Ask: 'Who can give an example of a thought that's all right to share in public?' 'What sorts of thoughts should we keep private?'

3. Introduction to this week's topic (10 minutes)

Ask students to brainstorm the different times they can think of when they 'need help' at school. Give some examples as a guideline, using the phrase, 'I need help when...' e.g. 'I need help when we have hard sums.', 'I need help when I don't know where to go.' If students focus primarily on the difficulties they have within a class, encourage them to think also of difficulties they might have at lunch and break-time. Help students to recognize that everyone finds something hard. Record responses on the board, either in writing or pictorially.

4. Topic-linked activity

ACTIVITY: HIDE THE MARBLE (10 MINUTES)

Materials: one marble

Group organization: free seating or standing in the group room

Ask one student to volunteer to be the Searcher. The Searcher's job is to look for a marble which will be hidden somewhere in the room. The

Searcher either leaves the room for a minute with a Group Leader or covers his/her eyes whilst the rest of the group hides the marble. When the Searcher returns (or opens eyes) he/she is not allowed to ask for any help and has two minutes in which to find the marble. After two minutes ask him/her to stop looking (unless they have already located the marble – which is unlikely if it has been hidden well). Then ask the group how we could make this task easier for the person searching. Encourage students to think about allowing the Searcher to ask for help. The Searcher then resumes the search but this time is allowed to ask the group questions about the whereabouts of the marble. The rest of the group can answer 'yes' or 'no', thereby helping the Searcher. Enable the student to find the marble (with the help of the supporting Leader if necessary). Ask the group what helped him/her to be successful. Reinforce the concept that we sometimes need to ask for help when something is difficult for us.

5 and 6. Role-play/drama and discussion (25–30 minutes)

The theme of the role-play is 'asking for help in class'. Ideally Leaders should carry out the first three role-plays.

ROLE-PLAY I

For the first role-play, one Leader plays the role of Teacher and the other of Pupil. The Teacher explains some work to the Pupil. The Pupil looks puzzled but does not say anything. He does not attempt the work set but sits looking out of the window, chewing his pencil, yawning, etc. After a couple of minutes the Teacher asks the Pupil how he is getting on. The Pupil just yawns. The Teacher becomes cross, asking him why he has not done any work. The Pupil says he does not understand what he has to do. At this point freeze the role-play.

DISCUSSION

Ask students the following questions:

> Why did the Pupil get into trouble?
>
> How does the Teacher feel?
>
> How does the Pupil feel?
>
> What can the Pupil do to help him get on with his work?

Encourage students to recognize that the Pupil could have asked for help. He could have said to the Teacher that he did not understand the work. Then the Teacher would have helped him with it rather than got cross with him.

ROLE-PLAY 2

For the second role-play Leaders again adopt the characters of Teacher and Pupil. This time the Pupil does ask for help but does so inappropriately. Whilst the Teacher is explaining the work the Pupil shouts out unhelpful comments, such as, 'I don't understand', 'This is too hard', 'Help me now'. The Teacher becomes cross with the Pupil for shouting when she is talking. She tells him that he will have to miss play if he keeps shouting out. Freeze the role-play.

DISCUSSION

Ask students:

> What happened in this role-play?
>
> How does the Teacher feel?
>
> Why is she cross/upset?
>
> How will the Pupil feel if he misses play?
>
> How could the Pupil ask for help in a good, sensible way?

ROLE-PLAY 3

For the third role-play, Leaders adopt the same characters. On this occasion the Pupil asks for help in a sensible way, after the Teacher has finished explaining the work. (Consider asking for suggestions from the group as to how a sensible pupil should behave.) The Teacher explains the activity to the Pupil, who then gets on well with his work. The Teacher congratulates him for working so well.

DISCUSSION

Ask students:

> What happened in this role-play?
>
> What did the Pupil do when he needed help?
>
> How does the Teacher feel?
>
> How does the Pupil feel?

EXTENSION ROLE-PLAY ACTIVITIES (10 MINUTES)

Provide students with the following scenarios to role-play in pairs or threes. Alternatively students can devise their own scenarios if this is appropriate. These role-plays focus on asking for help in an appropriate manner. Give an opportunity for students to rehearse the role-plays first for a few minutes before showing them to the rest of the group.

107

SCENARIOS

1. Shop scene: two people adopt roles of shop assistants and one person takes the role of a customer. The customer wants to buy some apples but can't find them. He has to ask the assistants where they are. One of the assistants tells him and he goes off to find them.

2. Class scene: one pupil adopts the role of Teacher and one of Pupil. The Teacher asks the class to draw a picture. One Pupil has not got a pencil. He puts up his hand and asks her sensibly for one. She gives him a pencil and he draws a picture. The Teacher is pleased with his work.

7. Closing activity (10 minutes)

ACTIVITY: MAKE A LINE

Materials: none
Group organization: according to game instructions

Students are asked to stand in a line according to different criteria. Start with simple, visual criteria such as lining up in order of height. Challenge students to form the line in under two minutes (or as appropriate). With older and/or more able students, use more subtle criteria that necessitate discussion between students, such as age, number of siblings and alphabetical order of surname.

8. Compliments (8 minutes)

With students still sitting in a circle, ask them to give a compliment about the person sitting on their left – something that person has done well in the session or more generally in school. This might include, for example, 'giving good answers', 'joining in role-play', 'sitting still', 'sharing pencils in class'. When compliments are given, record them on the pupil sheets.

9. Homework (5 minutes)

Students are to note on Homework Sheet 8.1 the occasions when other people needed or asked for their help. If possible, students should record why the person needed help and what their own response was. This activity should help students see that everyone needs help at some point and that it is sensible to ask for it when needed.

10. End session (2 minutes)

Praise students for completing the session and for working hard at the activities. Remind students that there are just two more sessions to go (if sessions are being followed in numerical order).

HOMEWORK SHEET 8.1: WHEN OTHER PEOPLE NEEDED OR ASKED FOR HELP

Today's date:

Why did the person need help?

I did…

What did the person do then?

✓

Model letter to parents/carers at the end of Session 8: Being confident to share views with others and to ask for help when needed

Date:

Dear Parents/Carers,

This week our topic began by students thinking about times when they have needed help at school. We found out that everyone finds something difficult and needs support from others at times. By playing an object hide-and-seek game, students discovered the benefits of help when an activity is especially challenging.

During role-play we looked at the different ways in which a student might ask for help. Students discovered that it is much better to ask for help with a difficult task than to avoid doing the task altogether. We also talked about appropriate ways of seeking assistance in school. These included waiting until the teacher or adult has finished explaining an activity before saying 'I don't understand' and using phrases such as 'Excuse me' to gain attention. Students were also encouraged to think about how they might ask for help when not in school, for example when out shopping.

For homework this week your child has been asked to record, by writing or drawing, occasions when other people have asked for their help. If your child has difficulty thinking of situations when they have been asked to assist another person, please help by providing two or three situations. These might include asking your child to help you tidy a room or prepare a meal. Where possible, ask your child to show you how to do something that he or she is especially good at. This will be confidence-boosting for him or her. The aim of the homework is for your child to recognize that everyone (including parents and teachers!) needs help at some point and that it is sensible to ask for help when it is needed. Your child should also start to recognize that he or she could play the important role of 'helper' too.

Best wishes,

Names of Course Leaders

- - - - - - - - - - - ✂ -

Dear Parents/Carers, please complete this section and return it with your child when he/she attends the next session.
How did your child manage the homework?

Does your child ask for help when he or she needs it at home?

☐ Always   ☐ Usually   ☐ Sometimes   ☐ Not often   ☐ Very rarely/Never

Tick box as appropriate.

Session 9

Target area: Recognizing and learning to resolve conflict (Skill Area 9)

Session aims and preparation

Key learning aims

Students: Recognize that people vary in their opinion and understanding of social situations, bring different experiences and motivations to situations and often have different wishes and goals

Understand that differences in opinion, understanding, experience and motivation can sometimes lead to misunderstanding and conflict

Develop strategies for analyzing confrontational situations and resolving conflict in a socially acceptable manner

General aims

Students: Appreciate diversity in people and accept human differences by developing greater tolerance of others

Increase their use of effective strategies to both avoid and cope with conflict

Develop further their listening skills

Link area of PSHE and Citizenship Curriculum

Students are able to respect human difference and form effective relationships

Materials needed

Information gathering sheets, bluish-green colour card (to be provided by teacher), Object Cards, magazines, A1 paper, crayons

Suggested additional materials

Hats and scarves for role-play

Session plan

1. Welcome to the group and warm-up activity (10 minutes)

ACTIVITY: SHARING INTERESTS

Materials: information-gathering sheets (Group Leaders to list suitable questions and photocopy one for each member of the group), bluish-green colour card

Group organization: students sit next to their partner at a desk or table, or with clipboards for writing/drawing

Students are organized into pairs. Within each pair students are assigned either an 'A' or a 'B'. Using the information-gathering sheet, As ask Bs questions about themselves, such as, 'How old are you?', 'Do you have any sisters?', 'What is your favourite food?' Bs respond as best as they can to each question. When A has completed all the questions on the sheet, B then becomes the interviewer and asks A the same series of questions. Student A responds, as best as he or she can. When all pairs have completed both interviews, Group Leaders ask for feedback from the different pairs. Leaders ask students questions to elicit individual differences, such as, 'Did anyone answer all the questions in exactly the same way as their partner?' As the answer is very likely to be no, ask students: 'Why do you think this is?' Encourage students to notice that although we are all at the same school and about the same age, we have many individual differences.

2. Recap on the previous session and on any homework set (8 minutes)

If the previous session was Session 8, ask students how they managed the homework exercise. Ask for volunteers to recall occasions over the previous week when someone needed their help. Remind students that all people, including people who look after us such as parents and teachers, need help at some point. Recap on the idea that it is much better to ask for help with a difficult job than not to do it at all.

3. Introduction to this week's topic (10 minutes)

Introduce the idea that sometimes we agree with our friends. Maybe we all like ice-cream or we all like watching football on TV. Sometimes we do not agree with our friends. Perhaps maths is my favourite lesson but my friend does not like maths. Perhaps my friend likes watching cartoons but I like watching nature programmes. We can disagree with our friends on lots of different things.

What happens when we look at various colour shades? Show students the bluish-green colour card and in turn ask each student what colour they see. Some may see the card as pale blue, others as light green, others as a dirty yellow. Who is right? Everybody might be right because it is such a mixed colour. Accept everybody's description.

What about another situation where there is only one ball but two groups of kids who want it?

4. Topic game (10 minutes)

ACTIVITY: FAVOURITES

Materials: Object Cards, pictures from magazines, large tally sheet
Group organization: students seated at a writing space, or with clipboards

Using the Object Cards from Session 3 and pictures from magazines, make a sheet with rows of foods, pets and other categories. Photocopy these for students and have them circle their favourite item in each category. The Group Leader introduces the activity saying: 'We would like to find out more about things you really like'. Pointing to the sheet, say: 'On each row there are pictures of different things. On the first row there are pictures of types of food. On the next row there are pictures of types of pets (continue to describe each category)'. Hand out a sheet to students and ask them to point to the first row. Say: 'Now circle your favourite food in this row'. When students have finished move on to the next row. Continue until students have circled a favourite item from each category.

When students have finished the task collect the sheets. Use the tally sheet to display the results. What do students notice about the results? Does everyone have the same favourite food? How many people like dogs as their favourite pet? How many people have chosen rabbits? Use these results to illustrate that we all have different tastes. We all have a different set of likes and dislikes.

5. Role-play/drama (25–30 minutes)

Provide students with the following conflict scenario. There are two groups of kids who each want to watch their favourite video. One group wants to see Spiderman. The other group wants to see Scooby Doo. There is only one video machine and the children cannot see the two videos at the same time. What can be done to avoid a fight?

Discuss possible solutions for this scenario with the group. These might include:

- They can toss a coin and whoever wins gets to watch their favourite video

- One group could watch their video first and the other group could watch theirs later

- No one gets to watch a video as they cannot decide on which one to see

- The Spiderman group get to see theirs and it's tough luck on the Scooby Doo group

- The teacher should decide

- They could all vote on it

Note the different ideas that students present and encourage them to think about the outcomes of their potential solutions. Draw a table on the board and record student responses. The table might look like this:

Solution – what could they do?	Outcome – what might happen if they do this?	Good or bad solution?
They could toss a coin.	The group that won would be happy. The other group might be upset but at least it's fair.	Good
The Spiderman group could destroy the Scooby Doo video.	The Spiderman group might end up watching their video but it wouldn't be fair. They'd get into a lot of trouble if the teacher found out.	Bad
The groups could have a race. Whoever puts their video in the machine first is the winner.	They would probably end up breaking the video. Then neither group could watch anything.	Bad
They could have a vote.	This way the group with the most students would win. If more students wanted to watch Spiderman then they should be allowed to.	Good

Divide students into groups of four or five. Select one of the 'Good' solutions for each group to role-play (or allow each group to select their own). Once each group has chosen a solution, Leaders work with the groups to help them develop a script for a role-play scenario. Each group then acts their scenario to the other.

6. Group discussion (5–10 minutes)

Following the role-plays, discuss with students:

- What was the problem here? (Encourage students to think about the concept introduced at the start of the session – that we all have different tastes and preferences and that this can cause us to disagree with each other.)

- Were one group right and the other group wrong? (Help students to understand that often in an argument, neither group is right or wrong. It is just that they do not share the same views.)

- Which solution do you think was fairest?

- Why do you think it was fairest?

7. Closing activity (10 minutes)

ACTIVITY: VISITORS

Materials: large sheet of paper (A1-sized), crayons
Group organization: students seated around the piece of paper, either at a large table or on the floor

Each student draws their own house or flat in a space around the edge of the paper. Houses should be drawn quickly and not be elaborate (they may be represented by a simple shape if drawing is hard for students or time-consuming). Explain to students that you can visit someone else's house by drawing a line from your house to theirs. The idea is that everyone is visited at least once. Students share one crayon between the group. The person who has just been visited takes the crayon and draws a line to another house. The owner of this house then takes the crayon and visits a different house. Continue until everyone has had at least one visitor. To add excitement to the task the group can be timed. How long does it take for everyone to have been visited at least once? The end product can be displayed in the group room.

8. Compliments (5 minutes)

With students still sitting in a circle, ask them to give a compliment about the person sitting on their left – something that person has done well in the session or more generally in school. This might include, for example, 'giving good answers', 'joining in role-play', 'sitting still', 'sharing pencils in class'. When compliments are given, record them on the pupil sheets.

9. Homework (5 minutes)

Ask students to note occasions during the week when they have a disagreement with somebody. This might be over things such as what game to play at break-time or what programme to watch on TV. Using Homework Sheet 9.1 at the end of this session, ask students to record (in writing or through drawings) what happened and what they did about it (the solution). If possible, students should record whether their solution was good (successful) or bad (unsuccessful).

10. End session (3 minutes)

Congratulate students for completing the session. If next week is the last week, remind students about the celebration.

HOMEWORK SHEET 9.1: DEALING WITH CONFLICT

What happened?	What did you do about it?	Was this a good or bad solution?
		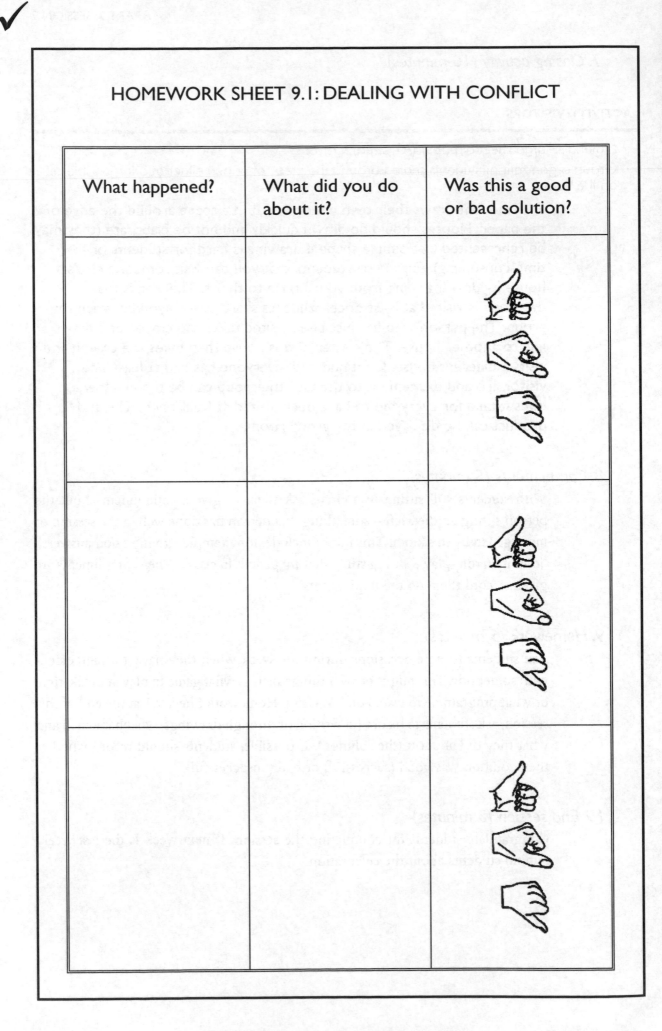

Model letter to parents/carers at the end of Session 9: Recognizing and learning to resolve conflict

Date:

Dear Parents/Carers,

We started this week's session by gathering information about each other. In doing so we discovered that, although we have many things in common with our peers (for example having the same number of brothers or being the same age), there are also many differences. For one person ice-cream is their favourite food; for another it may be pizza. Some students have brown eyes, others blue, and others green or grey. Students were encouraged to notice that, although we are all at the same school and about the same age, we have many individual differences.

We then found out that sometimes our individual differences can cause arguments and conflict. What happens if one group of children wants to see a Spiderman video and another group wants to watch a Scooby Doo video? There is only one video recorder so what can be done to avoid an argument? Students discussed possible solutions and their outcomes. They then selected solutions with good outcomes and role-played these. Following the role-plays we talked about whether the Spiderman or Scooby Doo groups were in the right and should have got their own way. We learnt that neither group was right or wrong. Because of individual differences we do not always want to do the same things as other people. We each have our own likes, dislikes, views and opinions.

This week for homework your child has been asked to make a note of the occasions when they have a disagreement with somebody. This might be over such things as what game to play at break-time or what programme to watch on TV. Using the Homework Sheet 9.1 on dealing with conflict please encourage your child to record (in writing or through drawings) what happened and what they did about it (the solution). Where possible help your child to decide whether their solution was good (helpful) or bad (unhelpful). Please remember to give plenty of praise to your child for his or her efforts.

Best wishes,

Names of Course Leaders

- - - - - - - - - - - - - - ✂ -

Dear Parents/Carers, please complete this section and return it with your child when he/she attends the next session.
How did your child manage the homework?

Does your child use strategies to help avoid or resolve conflict?

☐ Often   ☐ Sometimes   ☐ Rarely

If yes, please briefly describe:

Target area: Showing care and concern for others (Skill Area 10)

Session aims and preparation

Key learning aims

Students:

Appreciate that they can get along better with others if they show tolerance

Recognize the importance of being helpful and caring to others

Recognize the importance of considering other people's needs as well as their own

Start to view a situation from another person's perspective as well as their own, thereby understanding what another person's needs and wishes might be

General aims

Students:

Draw together the main themes from the previous sessions

Feel good about themselves

Care about one another

Show good social interactions with one another

Promote each other's as well as their own interests

Link area of PSHE and Citizenship Curriculum

Students build effective relationships by being able to put themselves in each other's shoes. They recognize their own and each other's feelings, initiate friendships, are able to listen, support and to show care. Students realize that their actions have consequences for themselves and others. They are honest with other people. Students voice differences of opinion sensitively and use sorry and thank you appropriately. They recognize worth in others and make positive statements about others. Students show respect by listening.

Suggested materials

Quiz sheets, hats and scarves for role-play

Session plan

1. Welcome to the group and warm-up activity (10 minutes)

ACTIVITY: FRIEND DETECTIVES

Materials: none

Group organization: students and Group Leaders seated on chairs arranged in a circle

Ask one student to volunteer to be the Friend Detective. Explain to students: 'In a minute the Detective will leave the group. Whilst he or she is gone we will choose a Special Friend. When the Detective comes back we will take turns at describing the Special Friend to the Detective without actually saying who the Special Friend is. The Detective's job is to work out who the Special Friend is. The Detective will have to listen very carefully to what the rest of the group are saying. Even the Special Friend can say something about themselves'.

The Friend Detective should go to another part of the room (if possible out of earshot of the group) with a Leader whilst the remainder of the group quietly decides whom the Special Friend will be. The group says 'Ready' when they have chosen someone. The Detective returns to the group and asks different members of the group to say something about the Special Friend. Group members must not mention the Friend's name and should try to avoid saying he or she. They should start each description with, 'This Special Friend...'. Examples might include the Special Friend's hobbies, things they are good at, their favourite foods, pets, places and in particular why they are special as a friend. Comments that relate positively to the person's character should be encouraged, for example, 'This Special Friend has a happy smile', 'This Special Friend is always kind to me' and 'This Special Friend often helps me out with hard work'.

Aim for each student to have a chance at being the Special Friend and change the person who adopts the role of Detective with each new round.

2. Recap on the previous session and on any homework set (8 minutes)

If the previous session was Session 9, ask students what they remember about dealing with arguments. Can they remember why arguments often start? Remind students that we are all different and like different things. Sometimes these differences cause arguments. Recap on the previous session's role-play. Ask: 'What happens when two people want to watch different things on TV?' Encourage responses such as, 'They could argue and fight about it' or 'They could find a solution'. Remind students: 'We know that people may like, and need, different things to ourselves. That means they may want to do something differently to the way that we do'. Say to students: 'I love swimming and am good at it, but my sister loves ice-skating and is very good on her skates. On Saturday we could either go swimming or skating. What shall we do?' Ask for some solutions from students. Help students understand that, 'We could have a big argument about whether to go swimming or skating. Alternatively we could come up with a solution. Perhaps we could go skating this weekend and swimming the next Saturday'.

Ask students to volunteer to feedback from the homework at the end of Session 9 (Homework Sheet 9.1). Did they get into an argument or conflict over the week? How did it start? Did they find a solution? Was their solution good or bad? Could they have done anything differently?

3. Introduction to this week's topic (10 minutes)

Ask students: 'What makes someone a good friend?' Encourage responses such as:

- 'helps me when I'm stuck'

- 'they play/muck about with me'

- 'they know when I'm feeling sad or angry'

- 'they try to make me feel better when I'm upset'

Help students notice that a good friend is someone who doesn't just think about himself or herself. A good friend also thinks about how other people are feeling. Tell students that a good friend understands that you like some of the same things but also like some different things. He/she understands that you do not always want to do what he/she does.

4. Topic-linked activity (8 minutes)

ACTIVITY: FRIENDSHIP QUIZ

Materials: quiz sheets (using the practice questions below and questions like those on page 121), enough for students to share one between two

Group organization: students are arranged in pairs and have access to a writing space (either a table or a clipboard)

Tell students that they are going to take part in a friendship quiz. They should work with their partner and decide together on the best answer for each question. Each question will be about friendship. Students must try choosing the answer that shows good friendship skills. Hand out quiz sheets to each pair. Then ask students to go to the practice question at the top of the page. Read this out to them:

'Bill likes playing football but is not good at it. You are having a fun football game during break time with your classmates. Bill asks you if he can join in the game. What should you say?'

1. 'No, because you're rubbish at football and will ruin our game.'

2. 'Yes, because you'll have fun playing with us.'

Remind students to think about what the friendly answer would be. Remember to think about how Bill is feeling.

Check students' responses and that they understand the quiz. Then read out the next four questions, giving time for students to discuss their responses. At the end of the quiz ask students what they noticed about being friendly. Encourage them to recognize the need to think about the other person, how they feel and what their needs are.

FRIENDSHIP QUIZ QUESTIONS (10 MINUTES)

You are eating lunch in the school dinner hall. You are sitting next to your friends. You see a new student sitting all by himself. Do you:

1. Ask him to come and join you at your table
2. Not bother to ask him because it's a hassle

You really want to watch a new TV programme. Your sister has a test tomorrow and wants to study for it. She finds it hard to study with the TV on. Do you:

1. Turn on the TV anyway because you really want to see this programme
2. Not turn the TV on and let your sister study

You see a student crying in the playground. She is not very pretty or popular and is always on her own. Do you:

1. Do nothing because you don't want to be seen with her
2. Go over to her and ask her if she is OK

You have a new pencil case with three new pencils in it. The boy sitting next to you does not have a pencil. You both need a pencil for your class work. Do you:

1. Do nothing because you don't want to share your new pencils
2. Ask him if he'd like to borrow one of your pencils

5. Role-play/drama (25–30 minutes)

There are three different role-play scenarios. Each scenario requires three Actors. The same, or different, Actors can be involved in each scenario. In all three role-plays, two students act as if they were having an interesting conversation (Actors A and B) and are joined by Actor C.

ROLE-PLAY I

Set the stage as a room with a door for Actors to walk in and out. Actors A and B stand together in the room and chat about something interesting. This could be any topic of their choice, for example a film they have both seen. Actor C enters the room and walks over to A and B. Both A and B

121

SOCIAL SKILLS TRAINING FOR ADOLESCENTS WITH GENERAL MODERATE LEARNING DIFFICULTIES

ignore C and continue chatting. C looks upset and walks away. Freeze role-play at this point. Ask observing students:

DISCUSSION

What did you notice?

How do you think Actor C feels?

Why do you think he/she feels that way?

ROLE-PLAY 2

Actors A and B stand together in the room and chat about something interesting. Actor C enters the room and walks over to A and B. This time both A and B are unfriendly and rude to C. They say things like, 'We don't want you to join us' or 'You don't know what we're talking about'. C looks upset and walks away. Freeze role-play at this point. Ask observing students:

DISCUSSION

What did you notice?

How do you think Actor C feels?

Why do you think he/she feels that way?

ROLE-PLAY 3

Actors A and B stand together in the room and chat about something interesting. Actor C enters the room and walks over to A and B. On this occasion A and B are friendly and welcoming to C. They tell C what they are chatting about and include him or her in their conversation. C looks happy and pleased to be part of the conversation. Freeze role-play at this point. Ask observing students:

DISCUSSION

What did you notice?

How do you think Actor C feels?

Why do you think he/she feels that way?

What was different about this role-play to the first two?

6. Group discussion (10 minutes)

Discuss with students ways of helping others. Ask: 'What you can do to help someone?' Encourage students to give responses such as 'be friendly, smile, play with the person, ask what they want, share a job, walk together, talk together'. Remind students that being a friend is thinking about the other person. What do they want? How do they feel?

7. Closing activity (10 minutes)

ACTIVITY: SQUEEZE A MESSAGE

Materials: none

Group organization: students and Group Leaders seated on chairs arranged in a circle

Students sit in a circle and all hold hands. One student sends a message to another member of the group, preferably a person whom he or she has not spoken to that day, by saying: 'I am sending a message to Duane' (if that is his name). He or she squeezes the hand of the person sitting next to him (on the left or on the right), who in turn passes it on. Duane announces when the message has reached him, and in turn sends a message to another student. Continue until all students have had a message sent to them.

8. Compliments (5 minutes)

With students still sitting in a circle, ask them to give a compliment about the person sitting on their left – something that person has done well in the session or more generally in school. This might include, for example, 'giving good answers', 'joining in role-play', 'sitting still', 'sharing pencils in class'. When compliments are given, record them on the pupil sheets.

9. Homework (5 minutes)

Students explore who are their friends. This should be done using the diagram of the Friendship Circle on the Homework Sheet for Session 10. The idea is that the individual is in the centre of the concentric circles, with names of closest family and friends in the inner circle and less close friends further out.

The Leader may also wish to repeat the sociogram described on page 33 as a way of comparing pre- and post-SST results.

10. End session (3 minutes)

Congratulate students for working hard at their social skills. If this is the last session, consider planning a meal, or an outing for the group, the following week. This will offer both a reward to students for participating in the sessions and an opportunity for them to practise skills learnt during the sessions. If possible, allow time to plan the meal or outing with the group, encouraging their participation. Consider asking parents and carers to the celebration.

HOMEWORK SHEET 10.1: FRIENDSHIP CIRCLE

Write names of family and close friends in the inner circle, and less close friends further out.

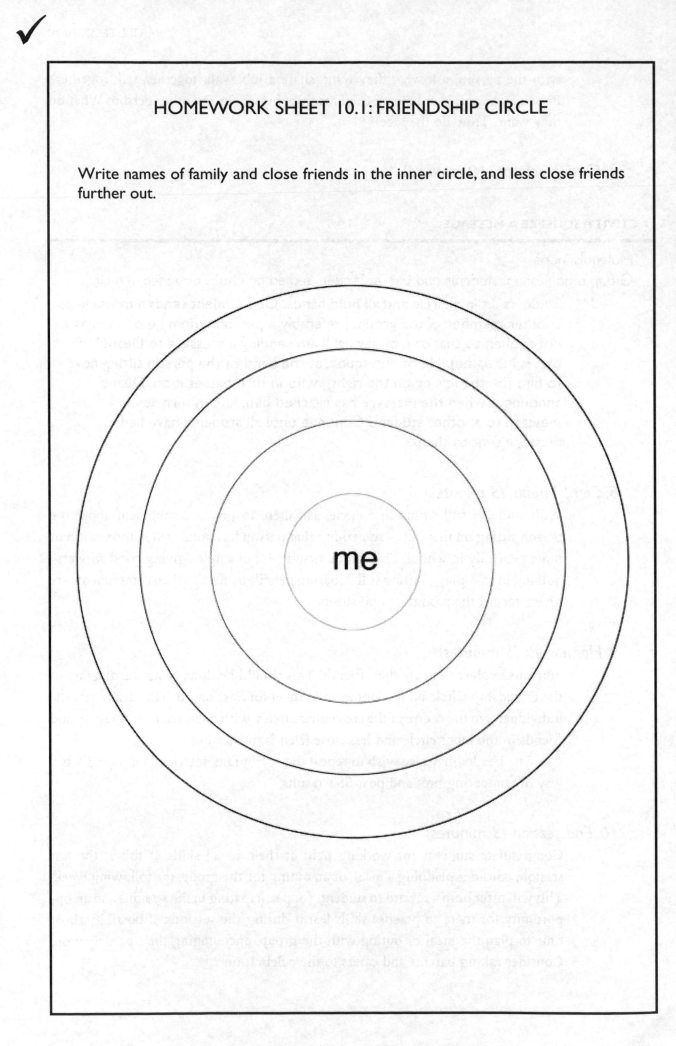

Model letter to parents/carers at the end of Session 10: Showing care and concern for others

Date:

Dear Parents/Carers,

We began our topic this week by talking about what makes someone a good friend. We recognized qualities that a friend has, for example someone who will help you out, whom you can have fun with, who knows when you feel sad and who tries to make you feel better. A friend thinks about other people as well as themselves. A friend understands that you may like or want to do different things to him or her.

Students took part in a friendship quiz and in pairs detected good friendship skills. They decided on the best 'friendly' response to problems such as seeing a new student eating lunch alone or wanting to watch TV when a sibling needs to study in quiet.

For role-play, students acted out scenarios in which two people chatted and either included or excluded a third person. Students thought about how the third person felt in each situation. We talked about how it feels to be excluded from a group and how we can make sure that our classmates do not feel left out.

For homework this week your child has been asked to complete the friendship circle on the homework sheet. Please help your child follow the guidelines on the sheet. Remember to give plenty of praise and encouragement for his or her efforts. Thanks for your support with this programme and for taking time to work with your child.

Best wishes,

Names of Course Leaders

·········✂···

Dear Parents/Carers, please complete this section and return it to school.
How did your child manage the homework?

Has there been any change in your child's social behaviour since they started the programme?
If yes, please describe some of the changes that you have noticed.

Index